PARADOX
OF CONSCIOUS HEALING

D1602653

R. Kelley Otani, MD

First published by Dog Ear Publishing
4011 Vincennes Rd
Indianapolis, IN 46268
www.dogearpublishing.net

ISBN: 978-1-4575-5114-7

This book is printed on acid-free paper.

Printed in the United States of America

CONTENTS

Dedication

To my teachers and to all the patients who found the courage to heal themselves.

Acknowledgments

There are so many people to thank for assisting in the creation of this book. I have great appreciation for the various teachers who are mentioned throughout the book. I want to express gratitude to Maureen Johnson, Diane Jones, and Joan Keegan for their initial editing and Mary Brentwood for her initial and final editing. I am grateful to my neurologist friend Matt Merliss for his input, continued support, and encouragement. I would like to thank Melinda Vernon and Leslie Kohler for their insight into the book publishing business and encouragement. I thank Neena Kaur and Warren and Sean Mikawa for helping me prepare my manuscript for printing. I wish to thank Feather River Health Clinic for giving me the opportunity to bring the principles of the book into a working reality. I am grateful to Stephanie McDonald and Berlanta Decroix for their coordination of the groups and program. I would like to express appreciation to Chaplain Brad Brown and Barry Pratt for volunteering their time in providing support and lessons for the groups. I also am grateful to Shannon Nicodemus and Amanda Mulrenam for their clinical support. Finally, I wish to thank my patients, who participated in the groups that continue to inspire and energize me in continuing my work.

PREFACE

"I wanted to change the world, but I have found
that the only thing one can be sure of changing
is oneself."

—Aldous Huxley

"Man's mind stretched to a new idea never goes
back to its original dimensions."

—Oliver Wendell Holmes

"The greatest discovery of my generation is that
human beings can alter their lives by altering
their attitudes of mind."

—William James

How can I help people to heal? My medical specialty is physical medicine and rehabilitation. I treat people who have received the best medical care but still have disabilities and suffering. Sometimes, illnesses can't be cured. They may actually get worse and lead to a lifetime of medication and treatment without resolution.

I wondered why certain people were more prone to illness or had a harder time healing than others. Two patients could have what is perceived to be the same illness and receive the same treatment, with one getting better while the other does not. Maybe the diagnosis is wrong and the symptoms have another root cause. Maybe we make the wrong assumptions that the origin of a diagnosis is physical when, perhaps, the origin is coming from another unseen source.

There is an interconnection between disease and suffering. Disease causes suffering, and a lifetime of suffering and emotional pain causes illness and physical pain. Recent research (see references; Felitti, Vincent J., et.al.) has shown that childhood trauma and abuse can cause a lifetime of unhappiness and disease.

Often, it isn't the disease that causes suffering for the patient but the impact the disease has in disrupting one's life and relationships with others. It can lead to the loss of a job, loss of identity, and loss of one's relationship with friends and loved ones. These losses lead to anxiety, depression, and social isolation. Life gets turned upside down. It is my job to help give patients as much of their lives back as possible—despite the disease and disability. I have spent my entire professional career trying to help heal people, but what I was doing just didn't seem to be enough. I knew there was more.

Are there other factors that assist in healing? Are there other unseen factors that also play a major role in affecting one's ability to heal? I would witness patients who had failed conventional medical treatment become healed by alternative treatment practices.

Who is this book written for? This book was written to provide an answer to these questions. I wrote this book for those who have tried everything conventional medicine has to offer but still haven't healed. I wrote this book to help people who have chronic disease deal better with life. This book is also written for people who have loved ones facing health issues. Finally, I wrote this book to help people who are healthy and want to prevent disease.

In my research, I discovered that the same factors that affect people's health can also affect their wealth and relationships. I looked at all aspects of healing: physical, mental, and spiritual. I expanded my knowledge to not only include my training in conventional medicine but also nontraditional healing practices involving the mind, body, and spirit. I learned about energy medicine. I studied different psychological theories and practices. I studied the works of Milton Erickson, who is one of the fathers of hypnotherapy; William Glasser, who developed reality therapy and choice theory; Tim Hallbom and Robert Dilts, who taught me Neuro-Linguistic Programming (NLP) as developed by Richard Bandler and John Grinder; Helen Schucman and William Thetford of *A Course in Miracles*; and Dr. David Hawkins, an enlightened physician and teacher who created the calibrated levels of consciousness and expanded the utilization of kinesiology in the pursuit of higher truth. I studied the teachings of Joseph Campbell, Tibetan lamas, and Caroline Myss, a medical intuitive. I grew up Christian but wanted to learn more about other religions, such as Buddhism and Taoism, to learn of spiritual healing. There are many stories about great avatars performing miraculous healing, and I wanted to discover their methods. In addition, I have spent time with indigenous healers: Grey Wolf, an Inuit shaman; Paah Pooh, a Native American woman healer; Tom Ballestieri, a Lakota medicine man; and Mark Saito, a Hawaiian *kahuna*.

Admittedly, I am not an expert in any specific discipline. My focus was in finding a common thread for all healing practices. Although specific rituals and procedures can be powerful, they can also be limiting. Oftentimes, what I found was that the true essence of a particular healing practice was buried under ritual. Great scientific discovery comes from questioning and breaking long-held dogma. It involves looking at a problem from a totally different perspective to find an answer. I attempted to look at the essential commonality that was embraced by all practices and teachings, despite their diverse approaches and rituals. I believe that looking at the commonalities in all things gives rise to truth and understanding.

As some scientists, including Stephen Hawking, have used unification theory to try and identify the commonalities of the scientific laws of the subatomic with the celestial, I have tried to find the truth in the different healing practices of the body, mind, and spirit to maximize healing.

I searched to discover ways to help my patients heal, but in truth, it ended up changing me to the point that I could no longer practice medicine the way I had been practicing. I walked away from my medical practice after twenty-one years and went on a vision quest. I walked alone in the desert and fasted for three days. I opened up all my "closet doors" and let my demons out: all the things I was angry about and all the things for which I felt guilty. With the release of the emotional pain, I experienced excruciating physical pain. It was a very humbling experience, and it took me a year to come back and practice medicine again—but this time, to practice medicine differently. I realized that to heal others, the healer has to heal himself (or herself) first. "Physician, heal thyself."

As I said in the beginning of this introduction, I spent my entire professional career trying to help heal people. I realize now that I had the wrong paradigm. I can't heal anyone. Instead of helping heal people, my goal is to help teach people to heal themselves.

I do believe in the power of traditional medicine and technology. The most effective healing, however, occurs with a holistic approach that addresses not only the body but also the mind and spirit. It involves treating the whole person instead of just the diagnosis. Patients that were thought incurable or chronic with conventional medicine have near-miraculous recoveries incorporating the holistic approach.

The first chapter describes what led me on this journey. The second chapter discusses the scientific evidence between the emotional pain and physical pain. The third chapter describes the physiology and power of the mind. Starting from chapter four, we enter the doorway into the mysterious and miraculous.

I organized the material in each chapter to gradually build the foundation for mind-body healing. Some of the selected chapters have exercises that reinforce some of the lessons and provide tools for everyday life. The material can be studied alone but is more powerful when studied with others in a group.

The final chapter describes my experience of putting the concepts into action. Groups were formed with my patients, who studied the lessons presented in this book. They often had remarkable results. Testimonials of some of the patients are presented at the end of this book.

I only ask that you stay open to possibilities. This book is about my healing journey, and I pray that it helps you with yours. *

* None of the material presented in this book is meant as a substitution for medical advice regarding your condition. Please consult your physician before proceeding with any of the elements presented in this book.

CHAPTER ONE

The Journey Begins

"If you can imagine it, you can achieve it. If you can dream it, you can become it."

—William Arthur Ward

"Do not go where the path may lead. Go instead where there is no path and leave a trail."

—Ralph Waldo Emerson

"Yes, I am a dreamer. A dreamer is one who can only find his way by moonlight and his punishment is that he sees the dawn before the rest of the world."

—Oscar Wilde

I t was later than I thought. I left the building and stepped out onto the street. There was a light drizzle, and the sidewalk and street reflected the dim light of the streetlamps. It's interesting how things can look so different at night. The comfort of familiarity during the day gives way to imagination in darkness. There was no traffic nor any sounds other than my footsteps. Home was only a few blocks away, and I walked at a leisurely pace when suddenly, I got a sense of another's presence. I was startled. I let my senses expand to locate and identify a source in the shadows. I kept walking and would occasionally catch a glimpse of a dark, sinister figure behind me, reflected through a storefront window. Every time I took a step, whether faster or slower, the dark figure would take a synchronized step seemingly in the hope of concealing his presence.

I felt a chill run down my back as I started to panic. My mind raced. What to do next? No one else was there but the two of us. My pulse quickened, and I started to break into a cold sweat as I tried to regain control of my brain and my emotions. Should I make a run for it, or should I stay and fight? Outwardly, I wanted to maintain an air of calm and self-assuredness. I wanted to pretend that I wasn't aware of his presence. I continued to walk calmly, then suddenly, after turning left around a street corner, I ran along the building and ducked into the nearest entryway, concealing myself in the shadow and waiting for him to come. I tried to quiet and slow my breath so I wouldn't be detected. As I sensed his approach, I jumped out and screamed at him. I grabbed him by the collar and dragged him into the light to see his face. In terror, I realized his face was my own.

It was a dream. I woke up startled and would think about it for months to come. What did the dream mean? Was I a closet schizophrenic? I realized I was becoming progressively more unsettled with what I was doing with my life. I was at a place I had dreamed of and worked toward since I was a teenager. I had studied hard and made many personal sacrifices. I felt like I had finally "made it." I was the medical director for a local hospital, had my own successful private practice, and had brought in other physicians to join my practice. I was married and had a son whom I loved. I had the big house, sports car, and swimming pool. I had power, success, and status. Something, however, wasn't right. I wasn't happy. I was a respected physician in the community, but in all honesty, I didn't feel like I was doing enough for my patients. Did the dream represent a suppressed side of me wanting to raise itself to my awareness?

How much do we really know of ourselves? We all have a shadow side. We have an image that we present to others and another side of ourselves that we knowingly keep hidden or deny. All the fears we avoid and desires we suppress. All the guilt, anger, and shame we bury under our addictive or irrational behaviors. True healing is having the courage to go into the shadow and find factors that may prevent healing. The act of confronting my shadow side is where my journey has led me. In my mission to help others to heal, I realized that I first had to heal myself by confronting my shadow side. This is the path of most healers. Many who are able to overcome illness and disease become healers themselves, because their experience brings them knowledge and understanding that they can then impart to others going through the same thing.

I am a medical physician who specializes in physical medicine and rehabilitation. I have cared for patients who suffered disabilities from illness or injury that prevented them from returning to their previous lifestyles. Those conditions include stroke, head injury, amputation, paraplegia, and other conditions that affected their strength, cognition, and function. In addition, I took care of patients who suffered from chronic pain. I was in private practice for twenty-one years and was a medical director for the hospital for twenty years. Over the last five years, however, I was starting to get burned out. In my specialty, I was known as a tertiary care physician. In other words, I was the one people would come see after all the other surgeons and physicians were finished with them. I would work with a team of therapists, nurses, psychologists, and other professionals to help my patients adapt to their conditions and become as functionally independent as possible. In the field of chronic pain, patients would come to see me after other physicians and specialists had tried everything else.

If a patient developed pain and had multiple lab and radiologic tests performed, but all the results were relatively normal, I would see them. If a patient developed pain and was found to have a definite physical cause for the pain, such as a herniated disc or a pinched nerve, and ended up having multiple procedures or multiple surgeries without any real improvement, I would see them. In other words, I would see patients who had failed all other modes of treatment, and I was their last hope.

Although I wanted to truly heal these patients, all I had available to me was medication or therapy that would only provide temporary relief. I felt I was doing nothing but covering up the pain with large amounts of medication, which did nothing to improve the person's quality of life beyond the basics of self-care. A few patients did well, but many came in complaining of increased pain—despite escalating doses of medication. They had exhausted all forms of treatment without success. They had depleted their life savings. They felt helpless, isolated, hopeless, and totally apathetic about life.

What if the patient is having symptoms, but all the diagnostic tests are negative? Is the person crazy? What if the patient has symptoms and has definite findings on diagnostic tests and undergoes appropriate treatment or surgery but still has no relief of symptoms? Is the patient crazy? Some people can have minimal or no findings and have pain, and others can have significant physical findings but have little or no symptoms. While doing my residency, I remember a research study in the early 1980's at the University of Washington studying a group of men in their forties who were asymptomatic and had active lifestyles. They were able to run, ski and play golf or tennis without physical limitations. MRI scans were performed of their lumbar spines, and the films were reviewed by a group of spinal surgeons, who did not examine the subjects and knew nothing of their history. Based on the MRI findings alone, 40% of those asymptomatic men were felt by the surgeons to be surgical candidates. Were the men crazy? Didn't these active men know they were supposed to be having pain based on the MRI findings?

There have been a couple of recent studies that have questioned the efficacy of some surgical interventions. One nationwide study reviewed the varied treatments of low back pain from all over the United States. The patients were selected for the commonality of symptomatology and radiologic findings. In one part of the country, the patients went in for early surgical intervention; in another part of the country, more conservative, less invasive, and nonsurgical interventions were used. In follow-up studies five years later, the research demonstrated there was no statistical difference in the outcomes of the surgical and nonsurgical patients (Birkmeyer and Weinstein, 1999).

Medical science and pharmaceuticals have had a tremendous impact on improving human health. Science has developed vaccines that have eliminated epidemics like small pox; antibiotics to treat bacterial infections; and surgery that unblocks heart or brain arteries. Despite massive increases in healthcare spending, however, life expectancy has not significantly improved. We continue to suffer from chronic diseases.

Chronic diseases are defined as conditions that are present longer than six months. As a Western-trained physician, I prescribed pharmaceuticals and physical modalities to relieve symptoms of chronic disease such as pain, anxiety, and depression. Patients would be stable only as long as they continued to take the treatment. Once patients stopped the drug or therapy, the symptoms would return. Sometimes, the symptoms would be controlled initially only to break through the treatment months later. Was I actually treating the disease or just masking the symptoms?

I began to wonder if there was another way of looking at chronic diseases than what had routinely been tried without long-term success. Albert Einstein once said that we can not solve our problems with the same level of thinking that created them. One has to evolve one's level of thinking to gain a different perspective and find a solution. The reason for this is that the solution may reside in other domains. Commonly in Western medicine, it is the symptoms (such as pain, anxiety, and depression) that are treated—rather than the actual root cause or pathology. The root cause, however, may not be in the physical domain.

We are all mind, body, and spirit. What is the connection between the mind and body in the creation of disease? Our health is dependent on three factors:

1. **Genetic**: what we are born with and diseases that we are inherently susceptible to.

2. **Environmental**: the **food we eat, the water we drink, the air we breathe, the stress we are under, and the toxins we are exposed to.**

3. **Behavioral: how we think, feel, and act.**

We have control of two of the three factors. Science has focused attention on identifying specific genetic loci that predispose us to disease. But how powerful is the mind? How is it that acupuncture has been used in pain control for major surgeries without anesthesia; a woman under hypnosis can be touched with a pencil that she thinks is a red-hot poker and then develop redness and welts; a patient with dissociative identity disorder can be clinically diabetic in one personality but asymptomatic in another personality; or a group of women are given what they think is chemotherapy and that one-third loses their hair—when what they actually received was a sugar pill?

There are terminal conditions that go into remission without any scientific explanation. Can patients be taught to heal themselves? I've described examples of patients who had symptoms without physical findings. Science can't explain the physical cause of essential hypertension, asthma, psoriasis, or autoimmune diseases. It is known that stress can lead to exacerbation of many diseases. Surgeons will tell you that a patient's attitude going into surgery plays a large role in affecting outcome and recovery. Renowned psychiatrist Dr. William Glasser was asked by an orthopedic group in Southern California to screen patients scheduled for spinal surgery preoperatively to see if identifiable psychological profiling could be used to improve outcome and recovery after surgery. Dr. Glasser concluded that whether the patient knew the exact moment of injury, felt "a pop" in his back at the time of injury, and how the patient perceived his life before the injury all played a large role in the success of surgery. If the patient felt he had a wonderful life and enjoyed his work before the injury, he did better after surgery than those who didn't enjoy life.

Cardiac patients who have positive attitudes and faith that their heart surgery will be successful have outcomes almost twice as good as patients who are pessimistic and have negative attitudes. Similarly, a study was performed by Dr. Steven Greer at King's College in England. The attitudes of fifty-seven women treated with mastectomy for early-stage breast cancer were studied for breast cancer survival. Women who believed they were going to overcome the disease or denied they even had the disease at all had a ten-year survival rate of 55%. Women who felt more helpless, hopeless, and fearful had a ten-year survival rate of 22%. It is known that workers who have negative opinions about their jobs are more likely to become injured at their work. A majority of heart attacks occur on Monday mornings. People hate their jobs enough that they are dying of a broken heart.

As a physician, I had been trained to look at the physical aspect as a cause for a disease, but I was having limited success in just treating patients for chronic conditions and pain. I wondered if a person could heal themselves through their mind and spirit. I wondered what it was that enabled a person who had a terminal condition to have a spontaneous recovery. If a person can heal themselves from cancer, can the same methods be applied in healing fibromyalgia or autoimmune disease? Why didn't people heal? What was I missing?

Disease comes from *dis-ease*, or a lack of ease or comfort. Health comes from the word *hale*, which means "to make whole." We are all body, mind, and spirit. Perhaps the answer wasn't in the physical realm but in the mental or spiritual. I had often heard stories about spiritual avatars, such as Jesus and Buddha, who were able to bring about healing without the use of drugs or surgery. That is what led me on my personal journey toward a greater understanding not only of others but also of myself.

To gain some insight into the mind, I studied the works of Milton Erickson, who was the father of hypnotherapy at the Milton Erickson Institute in Arizona, and the works of Virginia Satir, a great social worker and family therapist. I studied with William Glasser, one of the world's greatest living psychiatrists. I studied NLP (Neuro-Linguistic Programming) from Tim Halbom, Nick Leforce, and Robert Dilts.

When he came to this country from Japan, my grandfather helped build the Methodist church in Loomis, and I grew up Christian. I wanted to gain a broader perspective, however, by studying other religions. There had always been anecdotal reports of miraculous healing through prayer and faith, but I had no idea how it worked. I studied the works of Houston Smith, Joseph Campbell, Caroline Myss, Helen Schucman and William Thetford, Eckhart

Tolle, David Hawkins, and Adyashanti. I also was drawn to indigenous spiritual healers. I studied with Greywolf, an Inuit shaman. I met Tom Ballestieri, a Lakota Uweepee medicine man; Lench, a Yaqui teacher; and Mark Saito, a Hawaiian *kahuna*. I studied and learned from Tibetan lamas and monks and from the writings of Lao Tzu. I wondered if miraculous healing could be understood with a better understanding of science. I studied David Bohm, Albert Einstein, and Stephen Hawking for the religion of science.

A lifetime could be spent becoming an expert in any one discipline of study—from the history to the lineage to the rituals and philosophies. Humbly, I must admit I am not an expert of any specific discipline. That was not my purpose. My purpose was to learn about the essence and the context of each and to find the truth in the commonality they all contained. Through the commonalities, I would introduce concepts in mind and spirit that would help in self-healing. The mind-body approach promotes well-being and augments healing. It improves health through empowerment when an individual takes an active role in his or her own healing. When combining medical science with these mind-body concepts, healing can be maximized, and miracles can happen.

CHAPTER TWO

Disease and Stress

"When I look back on all these worries, I remember the story of the old man who said on his deathbed that he had had a lot of trouble in his life, most of which never happened."

—Winston Churchill

"There cannot be a stressful crisis next week. My schedule is already full."

—Henry Kissinger

"If you are distressed by anything external, the pain is not due to the thing itself, but to your estimate of it; and this you have the power to revoke at any moment."

—Marcus Aurelius

"Tension is who you think you should be. Relaxation is who you are."

—Chinese proverb

Nature Verses Nurture

There has been a long and ongoing controversy in science regarding the origin of illness. How influential is nature (or genetics) versus nurture (or environmental factors) on health and disease? Originally, it was thought all disease was caused by unseen spiritual entities (environmental factors) that caused miasmas. Then, it was the scientific belief that a predominance of diseases were inherited (genetic) and not amenable to change. Undoubtedly, genetics plays a major role in the makeup of exterior body features such as height, facial features, and eye color. Genetics also plays a major role in internal organ strengths and susceptibility to specific diseases. Some research has shown that 90% of all body anatomy and physiology is genetically determined. Twins separated from birth demonstrated the influence of genes by developing similar personalities and basic preferences—despite being raised in totally different environments. It was originally thought that many diseases such as cancer were predominately inherited.

Clearly, the environment also plays a role in health. Exposures to harmful toxins, heavy metals, radiation, organisms, or viruses have led to higher incidences of mental and physical developmental disorders, as well as diseases such as cancer. From the environment, the body requires supplemental molecules that it cannot produce on its own, including vitamins, minerals, essential fatty acids, and even sunlight. The lack of these exogenous molecules can affect health and lead to disease.

In nature, we see examples of plants and animals turning on or off parts of their DNA depending on the environment. With the change in seasons, we witness trees develop flowers and leaves in spring, change color in fall, and eventually drop off the branches during winter as the tree becomes dormant. The caterpillar forms a cocoon and eventually becomes a butterfly. An octopus or chameleon is able to change its appearance through camouflage. Certain toads, when exposed to the pheromones of a predator, will grow spines on their skin, and their offspring will also be born with skin spikes.

As mentioned, health is based on three factors; genetics, environment, and behavior. We are all genetically predisposed to have certain conditions, and exposure to environmental toxins can cause disease. We have yet to discuss, however, the health effects of our *behavior*. We can take control over how we act and can limit our exposure to unhealthy elements in the environment. There are indisputable studies demonstrating that maternal neglect or abuse during the first three years of life can lead to disease, mental disorder, and early death. If cancer is like other diseases, some researchers believe that environment and behavior may account for 85–90% of all diseases.

Mind-body medicine utilizes the power of the mind to significantly augment existing medical treatment or act as the primary mode of treatment in illnesses not responsive to other healing modalities. It requires an individual to actively participate in the healing process by changing toxic belief patterns.

It is not uncommon for a medication or surgical treatment to be effective initially, then after a few weeks, for a relapse to occur, requiring additional drugs or repeated surgeries only to have the symptoms recur again, creating frustration not only for the patient but for the medical provider as well. In medicine, there is a placebo effect that occurs in which an individual may have temporary or permanent relief of symptoms through a mode of treatment that arises from a patient's *expectations*, rather than as a direct result of the treatment itself. The response rate can be 30% or higher, comparable to many drugs and procedures. There are reports of individuals having spontaneous recovery from incurable or terminal conditions through drastic changes in lifestyle, belief patterns, or an unwavering devotion to a spiritual practice.

Healing the mind and body starts with understanding. First, one must understand the disease process from the pathologic perspective. Second, one must know the cause of the disease from an energetic perspective (i.e., from emotion and belief). Acute disease can be treated early and generally responds to conventional medical treatment. If the disease becomes chronic (over six months), other root causes for the disease should be explored. An acute disease that becomes chronic may be because of a wrong diagnosis, an initial symptom of a more systemic problem, or origination in the nonphysical realm. Chronic disease may make the body weak and unable to heal itself. Long-standing disease not only affects the body's physiology but the brain's neuro-pathways as well. Medicine and treatments that help alleviate the initial suffering are appropriate to calm the body and allow the mind to focus. As with Tibetan medicine, however, chronic disease may not be healed quickly enough to cure. The longer one has a disease, the longer it may take to heal and the more dedication is required from the patient.

Inflammation

Inflammation is a defense mechanism to keep the body safe. The body reacts to something it thinks is dangerous and attacks it. Somewhere in the body, an infection, toxin, or injury causing pain sets off chemical and cellular reactions that occur locally at the site and communicate with the rest of the body through electrical and chemical pathways. Multiple reactions take place that dilate blood vessels in the area to allow better access for cells to fight off the foreign invader. White blood cells (called macrophages) kill invading organisms and eat away dead or damaged cells and tissue. Other cells come in to help repair any damage and replace the dead cells.

Inflammation works well unless it mistakes something that is not a threat (benign) for something dangerous. Sometimes, the immune and inflammatory cells can become oversensitive and hypervigilant. In these cases, a large immune response to a perceived threat can be triggered by the smallest irregularity. The body can be so afraid of attack that it doesn't recognize the normal cells of the body and attacks them as if they were an enemy. That is the cause of autoimmune diseases such as lupus, asthma, and rheumatoid arthritis. Some people who have had traumatic or abusive childhoods grow up more afraid of life and of attack, making them more prone to autoimmune diseases.

Cancer

The body is a marvelous system of cells that work together as a community to sustain the life of the whole. Each cell in each organ has a specific job. No one cell is any more or less important than the others. In some cases, there are cells that no longer wish to work in conjunction with the rest of the other cells and just want to eat and make other cells just like themselves. They keep eating all the food and don't do any work or care what happens to any other cells except themselves. They multiply rapidly and cut off food and nourishment to the rest of the cell community. All the other cells in the body starve to death. These narcissistic cells are called cancer cells.

Cancer is the loss of the cell's ability to regulate growth and proliferation. The body is constantly replacing damaged cells or repairing them and taking out old molecules and replacing them with new molecules. Some scientists have said 98% of the atoms in the body are replaced every year, and the same could be said of cells in the body. Older or damaged cells are replaced by newer healthy cells. For example, stomach lining cells are replaced every five days; skin cells are replaced every month; liver cells are replaced every six weeks; and skeletal cells replace themselves every three months. Errors in factory cell production and cancer cell formation occur all the time. We all have cancer cells that get produced in our body throughout our lives. Lab tests are only able to detect cancer when the number of cells exceeds one billion. The defective cells and cancer cells are normally destroyed by the body's immune system. If the immune system is compromised, however, the cancer cells are allowed to grow unabated.

Recent scientific studies suggest only 10–15% of cancer is genetic mutation (NIH: National Cancer Institute). Samples of both cancer cells and noncancer cells were taken from cancer patients for genetic comparison. The study demonstrated no evidence of cancerous DNA in the healthy cells' DNA. Therefore, something happened to the normal cells to cause the genes to mutate and cause cancer. Researchers are now looking for the factors that cause the DNA to mutate. Chemical carcinogens, viruses, or ionized radiation in the environment can cause a disruption, affecting the growth control mechanism on the DNA. Traditionally, Western medicine has held the dogma that "once a cancer cell, always a cancer cell." Treatment by oncologists uses chemical agents and ionized radiation to kill all fast-growing and replicating cells of the body. This includes both cancerous and healthy cells that reproduce rapidly, such as blood cells, immune cells, hair cells, skin cells, and gastrointestinal cells. Normal, healthy cells are considered "collateral damage" in the war against cancer. The current scientific dogma that cancer cells cannot revert back to normal doesn't explain why some cancer survivors have complete remission of their disease. It has been shown that cancer cells in salamanders can back revert to normal (Fior, 2014).

What causes the body to underreact to infection and overreact to inflammation? In both Western and Eastern healing practices, disease is thought to be caused by resistance or obstruction. Obstruction or blockage of a body's chemical pathway that produces a necessary enzyme or hormone can lead to a malfunction of the body's metabolism or structure. A blocked artery can cause a stroke or heart attack. Increased resistance or obstruction in a nerve can lead to pain, numbness, or weakness. An obstructed bowel or kidney can lead to the accumulation of toxins in the body. In Chinese medicine, there is a natural flow of life energy that surrounds and runs through the mind and body called *qi* (pronounced "chi"). The energy running through twelve meridians, or channels, can become obstructed, causing diseases of any organ along that energy pathway. In acupuncture, the goal is to remove the obstruction of the flow of *qi* along these energy meridians.

In mind-body medicine, it is felt that resistance or denial of thought can lead to altered behavioral patterns that can affect health and lead to disease of the body. There is a crossover of disease from the mind to the body and from the body to the mind. From the mind-body perspective, aberrant mental states can be the root of many diseases. Treating symptoms with medications is similar to treating a fever without addressing the underlying infection. The antipyretic may work for a while, but the fever reemerges because the root cause still exists.

A physical illness or injury can lead to emotional distress such as depression, anger, fear, or anxiety. Unhealthy mental conditioning can affect physical health in a way that is as harmful as any physical illness. Depression can change the brain's neurochemistry and lead to forms of unhealthy behavior, passive or active suicide, addictions, and death. Stress is a psychological state known to cause many health problems. Stress impairs the immune system and makes one more prone to infection, autoimmune disease, and cancer. Stress is caused by inner conflict or resistance in the mind between what the body is doing, what the mind is thinking, and what the spirit wants.

Stress

The stress response has been present in man and animals throughout time. The brain and body have a built-in stress response to react to perceived danger. Think of early man confronted by a saber-toothed tiger. He had to have immediate focus, strength, and speed. The brain affects the body through neurologic and hormonal signals to undergo physiologic changes. The goal is either to fight for one's life or to escape from the threat as fast as possible. The changes to the body involve diverting all the energy toward the muscles and narrowing brain focus. The stress response is mediated through the autonomic nervous system and the release of adrenaline and natural steroids (such as cortisol and other glucocorticoids), which change the body and brain functions when confronted by a perceived threat. The autonomic nervous system gives the body a burst of energy and strength. Blood flow to the muscles and the brain increases by 400%, respiration rate increases to improve oxygenation, and energy stores are released. The stress response is beneficial for survival for a short duration.

Stress can be addicting. One can intentionally put oneself in stressful situations. We even pay for temporary stress on roller coasters and other thrill rides at amusement parks. We pay to watch action and horror movies. Some take pleasure in activities that may cause disability or even death. They engage in dangerous work or sports such as rock climbing, mountaineering, and bungee jumping, or in dangerous relationships because it gives the participant a "rush." Physiologically, adrenaline and cortisol cause the heart to pump faster and harder and the muscles to expand in tense readiness. "Adrenaline junkies" say they feel they are "cheating death" and that it makes them "feel alive." With the narrowed focus of the brain, people are less troubled by distracting negative thoughts of the past or the future, and while they are doing the activity, they feel "more present." Spiritually, the "rush" and sense of greater aliveness comes from transcending fear and gaining a higher energy level of courage.

Modern-day stress, however, is oftentimes much different. There are no longer saber-toothed tigers but saber-toothed bosses, ex-spouses, or co-workers who we may have to continue to interact with for many years. We voluntarily keep ourselves in conditions of constant stress. Stress can arise from physical or emotional sources. Heavy commuter traffic, worry about finances, anger at work, or dysfunctional personal relationships can all cause constant psychological stress. We keep ourselves in positions of constant stress because of perceived necessity, desire for the rewards, or fear of loss.

It has been scientifically proven that prolonged stress has a deleterious affect on health. Stress has been shown to contribute to increased susceptibility to infection, hypertension, heart disease, and problematic hormonal (endocrine) levels. Stress arises in the mind from a perceived threat or a sense of helplessness.

When the body and brain are exposed to continuous stress, they begin to break down. "Stress impairs neurogenesis (brain regeneration)," says researcher Peter Ericksson at the Sahlgrenska University Hospital in Sweden (Ericksson, 1998). In addition, an inundation of stress hormones rips apart synapses that connect brain cells to one another.

Dr. Tessa Rosebloom found that chronically stressed fetuses in utero had poorer health during their lives. Brain chemistry is affected, leading to various mental diseases and personality disorders. Looking at the DNA molecule, there are portions of repetitive genetic molecules that act to hold the DNA strand together. Called telomeres, they are similar to the plastic ends of shoelaces. As one ages, the telomeres get shorter, and the ends of the DNA molecule get more frayed. This leads to the molecule sticking to itself, causing mutation and cell death. Long duration of stress has been shown to shorten telomeres of DNA chromosomes and decrease life expectancy by six years (Epel)

In an attempt to better understand the effects of chronic stress on humans, scientists have studied the effects of stress through animal studies. Evolutionarily and genetically, primates are the closest relatives to humans. It is known that constant stress can kill brain cells. Stanford University researcher Dr. Robert Sapolsky studied stress and stress hormone levels in baboons in Africa. Baboons have a social hierarchy, and it was discovered that rank in that hierarchy affects stress level. Lower-ranking subordinate and passive baboons have more stress hormones than higher-ranking primates in the same group. Other studies have shown monkeys of low rank develop accelerated atherosclerosis.

In humans, there is a relationship with status and stress as well. In the Whitehall studies, Michael Marmot, professor of epidemiology and public health and head of the International Center for Health and Society at University Hospital in England, studied 10,000 British civil servants to learn the effects of human social hierarchy on stress and health. He and his team found a dramatic four-fold difference between the top and the bottom of the civil servant hierarchy. The study established controls for such variables as smoking, diet, blood pressure, exercise, income, and social support. They found that a gradient formed: As one moved further down in rank and class, there was a progressive increase in disease. The lower hierarchal workers demonstrated a progressively higher risk for cardiovascular disease and sick leaves. The researchers found that the lawyers and doctors, who were just one step below the top-ranking executives and professionals, had twice the incidence of disease as the highest echelon. It was concluded that the lack of ability to determine one's destiny played a major role in the development of stress and disease.

Stress can affect fat distribution in the body. Dr. Carol Shively, a professor of pathology at Wake Forest School of Medicine, has studied the effects of social stress on the body and brain. The female monkeys in her study were fed a Western-style diet that contained high levels of fat and cholesterol. The monkeys were part of a community that tended to create a social hierarchy from dominate to subordinate. The lower-ranked monkeys were often the target of aggression by the higher-ranked monkeys. The subordinate monkeys were not allowed to participate in the daily grooming activities as often as the dominant monkeys. Dr. Shively measured dopamine levels and brain function in stressed monkeys and found subordinate monkeys had less dopamine on their PET scans. She also found there was greater fat accumulation in the abdominal cavity of the subordinate monkeys than in the dominant female group. It tended to be a different type of adipose that was associated with plaque formation in the arteries and led to a greater risk for heart disease. This corresponded to the findings in the Whitehall Study that human weight gain associated with constant stress affected the distribution of fat more around the abdomen than other areas of the body. A study published in the August 2010 edition of *Archives of Internal Medicine* studied more than 100,000 people from 1997 to 2006. Lead author Eric Jacobs and his team found that men and women with the biggest waistline had twice the risk of dying over a decade—even if their overall weight was normal. Other researchers have found links between waist size and dementia, asthma, and breast cancer.

Constant stress has also been shown to impair the body's immune system. Originally, stress was felt to be the primary contributor to ulcers. In the 1980s, H. pylori bacteria was discovered in those who suffered from ulcerative disease. The gastrointestinal tract, however, is normally colonized with vast numbers of bacteria, and subsequent studies showed the H. pylori bacteria were normal inhabitants in many individuals who never developed ulcers. Therefore, it can be concluded that stress can impair the body's immune system in its ability to fight off infections from normal body flora. Similarly, stress may impair immune cells' ability to destroy cancer cells.

Some animal researchers have studied the effects of stress on the brain. Dr. Bruce McEwen, a professor at Rockefeller University, was interested in the effects of estrogen and glucocorticoids on the brain. He studied the effects of stress on rat brain anatomy. The hippocampus of the brain converts sensory information and interpretation into memory. Rats that experienced constant stress had comparatively smaller areas of the brain's hippocampus than those not exposed to constant stress. Studies have corroborated these findings of memory impairment in humans who experience constant stress. Long-term stress also seems to affect the brain's ability to perceive pleasure. Dopamine is one of the pleasure neurotransmitters in the brain that provides a sense of joy.

With chronic stress, the body is in a catabolic (breaking down) state, and body energy stores are depleted. 43% of all adults suffer adverse health effects from stress, and 75–90% of all doctor's visits are for stress-related illnesses. Stress costs American industry more than $300 billion annually (WebMD: The Effects of Stress on Your Body). Initial symptoms of chronic stress include insomnia, chronic headaches, irritability, forgetfulness, and susceptibility to infections. Later, chronic stress influences the development of conditions such as depression; hypertension; diabetes; allergies; memory problems; asthma; skin conditions; hair loss; heart disease; thyroid dysfunction; obsessive-compulsive or anxiety disorder; sexual dysfunction; drug, tobacco, and alcohol abuse; obesity; tooth and gum disease; ulcers; and, potentially, cancer.

Our bodies all have a genetic predisposition for developing certain diseases. Some are more prone to heart disease; others are more prone to arthritis or cancer. It is stress that uncovers that weakness. The physical aspects of the prevention and treatment of stress and disease are as follows:

1. Exercise decreases the white cells (body defense) from becoming sticky and decreases inflammation and disease response. It also decreases stress hormones and increases endorphins (naturally produced pleasure- and pain-reducing molecules) that improve mood, sense of well-being, and brain function.

2. Diet improves brain and body functioning with proper nutrients. A proper diet that eliminates toxins (including alcohol, smoking, and caffeine) improves the tolerance of chronic stress. Decreasing processed foods and sugars improves energy and mood.

3. Environmental factors that cause stress can be reduced by allowing time for relaxation and meditation. It is about finding balance and making time to nurture yourself. Allow yourself to socialize and spend time with friends.

As we learned, however, stress isn't about physical factors but our *reaction* to the physical factors. Treating stress with just physical techniques will provide limited benefit. People react to stress differently: Two people can experience the same event but experience a different response.

Stress comes from conflict and resistance. Resistance occurs in the mind through fear, anger, or pride. As we discussed with Eastern medicine, the resistance in the mind leads to resistance and blockage of energy flow in the body causing the accumulation of toxins, organ dysfunction, and disease. The mind thinks by fighting or resisting something, it overcomes and wins. The antidote is to surrender. The spirit knows to surrender and let the energy flow, resulting in rebalance and health. If the root of the stress is in the mind, this is where we have to go to uncover the cause and treat it.

CHAPTER THREE

Body, Brain, and Consciousness

"Our bodies are our gardens, to the which our wills are our gardeners."

—Shakespeare

If the body is feeble, the mind will not be strong."

—Thomas Jefferson

"Good for the body is the work of the body, good for the soul the work of the soul, and good for either the work of the other."

—Henry David Thoreau

"The human body is vapour materialized by sunshine mixed with the life of the stars."

—Paracelsus

W here did life come from? In 1953, the DNA molecule was decoded by scientists James Watson and Francis Crick, for which they received the Nobel Prize. Crick believed that life was created from a primordial ooze: a collection of different elements and chemicals that was struck by lightening. Along with fellow scientist Stanley Miller, Crick performed numerous experiments to get the right ingredients under the ideal likely conditions that would have produced life. When I attended a biochemistry class at UC San Diego, Dr. Miller would lecture, perform mathematic calculations, and derive chemical formulas on how the creation of life from non-life likely took place. Despite their great scientific intelligence and zeal, however, the scientist's efforts to reproduce the genesis of life were spectacular failures. Over the years, numerous additional attempts at creating life from non-life have been equally unsuccessful. Clearly, there is a missing ethereal ingredient that contributed to the formation of consciousness and of life. From a biologist's perspective, the definition of life requires two qualities: 1.) consciousness (i.e., awareness of self and surroundings) and 2.) the ability to reproduce itself. The simplest single-celled organism has the consciousness to be able to discern and move toward what is desired within its surroundings (such as food or for reproduction) and moves away from what is dangerous and should be avoided. The only two known exceptions are viruses and moss. The evolvement and creation of human life is even more miraculous.

After human conception, the single fertilized egg multiplies to 100 trillion cells that all contain the same DNA molecule. In each cell, however, portions of the DNA molecule are turned on and other portions are turned off, based on the type of specialized organ they are to become. How cells know what to do and how to evolve seems incredible. Some cells become lung cells that bring oxygen from the environment to the rest of the cells. Gastrointestinal cells help break down food material from the environment into fuel and nourishment that the other cells can use. They also act as "garbage men" to eliminate solid waste from the body. Blood cells carry oxygen and provide body defense; skeletal cells provide the framework and physical support; muscle cells assist in locomotion; and nerve cells direct and communicate with the rest of the body.

In animals (including humans), the brain is the control center for the rest of the body and directs the body toward a given action. A more in-depth description of the way the brain works is discussed in Appendix A. The brain receives stimulating input from senses inside the body and the basic five senses outside the body. These external sensory nerves are smell, taste, hearing, seeing, and feeling. The brain places value (emotion) on the sensory information, decides if it is something that is desired or feared, and then directs the body's actions toward or away from the stimulus. The communication from the brain to the body occurs through electrical (nerve) and chemical (hormonal) pathways. With each experience, thoughts are attached to an emotion, and actions are taken. The experience, emotion, and corresponding action are recorded as memory and stored in the cerebral cortex (memory bank). Later, when a similar situation occurs, thought and emotion are recalled from the memory and direct the body to act in the same way.

The Autonomic Nervous System

Once the brain has decided on a course of action for the body, the autonomic nerves regulate and synchronize the body's organs through nerve and hormonal transmissions. This leads to a change in physiology to better adapt the body to achieve its desired action. The autonomic nervous system regulates the body's temperature, heart rate, blood pressure, digestion, etc. It becomes activated when something in the body or the environment is perceived as desired or as a threat. The autonomic nervous system has two different systems: the **sympathetic** and the **parasympathetic**. If the stimulus is perceived as being something that is desired (such as food or a mate), the parasympathetic system becomes activated. Things desired lead the parasympathetic system to decrease the heart rate and blood pressure, increase the digestive system, and provide a sense of calm. The sympathetic system becomes activated when the body perceives a threat. It is otherwise known to provoke the body's fight-or-flight response. The sympathetic system will speed up the heart rate, pumping more blood, energy, and oxygen to the muscles when strength is needed and dilate the pupils of the eyes to increase alertness and vigilance. Once the perceived threat has passed, the parasympathetic system takes over to slow the body back down to rest.

Stress and the Mind

Stress activates the sympathetic nervous system. The stress can come from the environment, either from a perceived threat or a desire for something that can't be obtained. Stress can come from the body because of pain or from the mind because of its perceptions. Perceived stress can come from other people through disagreements or from the self, with its inner conflicts. There may not even be a physical reason for stress, but the mind and body react as if there were a threat. Stress can be caused by perceived distortions in time. We live with schedules and deadlines. We experience the emotions from future or past events. Emotions of worry, desire, or fear cause stress by living in the future. Guilt, anger, and grief cause stress by living in the past. What might be highly stressful for one person (e.g., a fear of spiders, heights, or public speaking) may have little affect on someone else. Stress comes from one's values, beliefs, and points of view. Even the physiologic affects of subordination are just a state of mind. Stress comes from a perspective of win/lose. Dr. David Hawkins states,

"Stress is resisting what we do not want and not stress is getting what we want. The problem is within oneself."

Pain

Pain is not experienced in the body. If I hit my thumb while hammering a nail, in truth, the pain is not experienced in the thumb. Phantom limb syndrome is a common condition in which a person with an amputated arm or leg will still experience feeling and pain in the limb despite the fact that the limb is no longer there. Pain is not even experienced in the brain. If one were to do a craniotomy and touch the brain, it would not feel pain. Sensory nerves send information from the body to the brain, where the signals are interpreted as pain. There is not only the physical sensation of pain but also the activation of emotions such as fear, frustration, or anger. Pain associated with negative emotion magnifies pain perception. The greater the negative emotional reaction, the greater the perceived pain. If the pain is severe or long-lasting, this causes the mind to stress, which keeps the sympathetic nervous system activated all the time.

The Brain Versus Consciousness

A common misconception is that we are our bodies. As we learned with phantom limb syndrome, the body cannot experience itself. A foot cannot experience itself as a foot. An arm cannot experience itself as an arm. In our society, so much of our ego-based self-esteem is based on how we appear to others. Many have had modifications, augmentations, or subtractions to their body in the hope that those changes will bring greater happiness by making them more attractive to others. Life and life situations always change with time, and outer beauty is impermanent. Individuals who identify themselves as their bodies will, with time, eventually experience the suffering of change. As a rehabilitation physician, I treated many patients who had major physical losses and disabilities, including loss of limbs, paralysis, or disfigurement. Patients with those conditions who identify extensively with their bodies tended to experience more severe depression and suffering, and their functional outcomes were less successful. Those who knew that they weren't their bodies had a better sense of who they were and were able to adapt more quickly to their new condition—and more capable of leading more productive lives.

The second misconception is that we are our brains. Reductionist scientists have always equated the physical nature of the brain with the nonphysical nature of consciousness. Like Drs. Crick and Miller, they believe consciousness is made up of neurons and other supporting cells that operate through interconnecting electrical circuitry and chemical reactions responding to external or internal sensory signals to produce the most appropriate bodily response. I wouldn't advise, however, that you dissect your brain to find the "you" in there. Science and medicine tried unconvincingly to explain emotions such as fear, love, and anger as just combinations of neuron-energetic pathways. If we were our minds and thoughts, we wouldn't have the awareness of what we were thinking or feeling.

The brain is thought to be the storage center for all memories. Certain memories are stored and different bodily activities are controlled by specific areas of the brain. Clinically, however, it is noticed that when a portion of the brain is removed or damaged, memory of different times in one's life remains intact, giving credence to a more holographic model of the brain. An explanation for this phenomenon would be that the essence of who we are transcends the physical. The brain is like the hardware of a computer, but it doesn't determine the running of software programs. This is the realm of consciousness.

Consciousness

Science tells us there is a connection between magnetism and electricity. All electrical currents run a magnetic field, and all magnetic fields run an electrical current. Almost everyone has had the experience of pulling clothes out of the dryer that have electrostatic energy. You can, at times, hear the electrical sparks as clothes are pulled apart. The clothes cling to themselves, to other clothes, or to your body because of the magnetic energy associated with the electric energy. The body is known to operate on ionic and electrical energies. Consciousness is an energy that is similar to the magnetic field that directs the brain and leads to the body's actions. It is not *in* the body; it comes from the field that *surrounds* the body. There have been scientific experiments done on salamanders (amphibians that have the ability to regenerate a limb or other amputated parts of the body). The research has shown that there is a subtle electrical or magnetic current that surrounds the area of amputation and directs the regeneration. Disruption of this energy flow from external energy currents greatly impairs the healing process. Consciousness may be an imprinted energetic field that surrounds, coordinates, and directs the growth of body organs. Like a magnetic field surrounds the body like a energetic aura, most of us had experienced. We can sense another person's emotional energy and feel the emotion a person is feeling—even without them saying anything. We can have the awareness of anger or the intuition of an unsavory intention that makes us want to avoid a person. We can be attracted to the radiating energy from someone with "animal magnetism."

The nonphysical nature of consciousness is analogous to the picture on a television set. The components, the picture tube, and the electrical circuitry are all comparable to the physical nature of the brain. The picture that appears on the screen is not physically *in* the television but is a transmission from a nonphysical source. If the television is turned off, the transmissions are still present but are no longer received by the television. Our thoughts and the energetic frequency of our consciousness define what channels or programs come in on the television and what appears on the television screen. What appears on the television screen is what other people see in us.

The Power of the Mind

It is now realized that the brain is more dynamic and flexible than previously imagined. An understanding of the full potential of the brain is just now being studied, with new excitement about its possibilities. We are capable of new learning and behavioral changes, both of which can have an impact on changing our brain pathways and chemistry. These will give us the ability to manifest beneficial effects on our body's health and on our relationships.

Can simply changing our perception change our health? We have previously discussed the affect of subordination on stress and illness. Ellen Langer is a psychology professor at Harvard and has done extensive research in the field of psychology and health. She and her student Alia Crum studied the effects that our beliefs have on our physical bodies. Dr. Langer observed hotel maids and the amount of physical work they did on their jobs. They would almost constantly be active cleaning and carrying heavy and cumbersome equipment up and down endless hallways. She did a survey of eight-four maids at seven different hotels and found that 67% of the maids felt they didn't exercise regularly and more than a third said they didn't get any exercise at all. "Given that they exercised all day long (at work), that seemed to be bizarre," Dr. Langer said. She measured the maids' body fat, hip-to-waist ratio, blood pressure, body mass index, and weight. All parameters were consistent with the maids' perception of a sedentary lifestyle, rather than the actual amount of exercise they were performing. She divided the maids into two groups. One group of maids was made aware that with their work, they were, in actuality, far exceeding the surgeon general's recommendation for an active lifestyle. Dr. Langer also calculated and made the group aware of the calories they burned throughout the day. The second group was not made aware of any of this information. After a month, the group that had a change in mindset demonstrated not only a 10 mm Hg drop in systolic blood pressure but also weight loss and changes in hip-to-waist ratio. In short, they were significantly healthier. The second group demonstrated none of these physical and physiologic changes.

There have been other studies demonstrating the power of mind over matter. In his book, *The Placebo Response: How You Can Release the Body's Inner Pharmacy for Better Health,* Howard Brody, director for the Institute for the Medical Humanities at the University of Texas, tells of a study in which asthmatic patients were given a drug known to exacerbate asthma but were told that the drug would *improve* their asthma. A significant number of the patients said the drug improved their asthma and had objective improvements on their pulmonary function studies.

The mind has the capacity to change how we perceive things, change our body and physiology. The study of consciousness in healing is the new frontier of scientific investigation.

The mind, body, and spirit are all interconnected but not synonymous. Acute diseases that are physical in origin but lead to emotional sequela (such as fear, grief, or depression) are cured by treating the root physical cause. Treating just the physical manifestations of a disease that originates in the mind can provide some benefit, but the underlying condition remains and may manifest itself in other physical ways. The mind is more powerful than the body. The mind tells the body what to do. Without the mind, the body just functions without action—like a patient under anesthesia or in a coma.

There is something even more powerful, however, than the mind and its consciousness. That is *awareness.*

CHAPTER FOUR

Awareness

"Let us not look back in anger, or forward with fear, but around in awareness."

—James Thurber

"The most beautiful thing we can experience is the mysterious. It is the source of all true art and science."

—Albert Einstein

"Knowledge comes from adding something every day. Wisdom comes from removing something every day."

—Lao Tzu

While I was researching and writing the rough draft of this book, my mother wanted me to go to her church and listen to a guest speaker, Captain Gordon Nakagawa, USN. Like Senator John McCain, Nakagawa was a naval aviator who was shot down during the Viet Nam war and was held captive in a concentration camp. He and the other prisoners of war were subjected to psychological and physical torture to try to break them down. Sometimes, the prisoners were so demoralized that they became apathetic and just gave up. Nakagawa talked about the strategies he used to survive the experience. After his lecture, I told him that many of the strategies he had used to survive his prisoner-of-war experience were the same ones I discuss in this book. The first strategy he used was to always look for an escape—no matter what. This is *awareness.*

I remember reading about a research experiment at the University of Pennsylvania in 1967 involving two groups of dogs. One group of dogs was restrained in a locked cage and repeatedly shocked for several days. A second group of dogs was not restrained; the cage door was left open, but they were also shocked. These dogs ran around the cage trying to avoid the shocks and were eventually able to find the open door and escape. A few weeks later, the experiment was repeated. The second group of dogs were again placed in the cage with the door left open. The dogs had learned from their previous experience to run out of the cage to avoid the shocks. The researchers then put the first group of dogs in the cage, but this time did not restrain the dogs. Rather, they left the cage door open and shocked the dogs. What did the dogs do? They stayed and took the shocks. The dogs couldn't see that they could escape the shocks at any time. This is "learned helplessness" and is the same phenomenon that happened to the prisoners of war. This is also what happens when we have a disease we can't overcome. When we give up, we lose our awareness. We live our lives in conditions of suffering in our "belief" cages and think there is no escape. It is only through increased awareness that we can open our minds to new possibilities.

Lao Tzu of the *Tao Te Ching* said, "Those who think they know … don't know and those who know they don't know … know." In other words, a person who thinks they know everything is unable to learn anything new. A person who knows that they don't know, however, is open to greater awareness.

We have come to expect science to have the answers to all the world's problems. Despite the great advances in science and medicine over the centuries, however, there is a consensus that what has been discovered is only a small portion of all there is to know (Figure 1).

Physical science defines *matter* as what makes up all substances: solid, liquid, and gas. Substances, or physical matter, can be defined as everything from a pencil to a tree, a mountain, water, air, clouds, and all the stars in the sky. All of our scientific laws are based on this 4%, but there is much more to know. *Dark matter* accounts for 22% of all matter that exists. It is not observable but is the force that holds everything together. Dark matter is thought to consist of subatomic particles, which account for gravity and govern the rotation of planets and galaxies. It seems paradoxical that subatomic particles even smaller than an atom would have the power to form orbiting galaxies. There is something even greater, however. Science tells us the massive *dark energy* is observable but inexplicable and so powerful that it is able to drive apart the entire universe at an ever-increasing speed. It accounts for 74% of all that exists. Scientists are aware of and able to observe dark matter and energy but have little understanding of how they work.

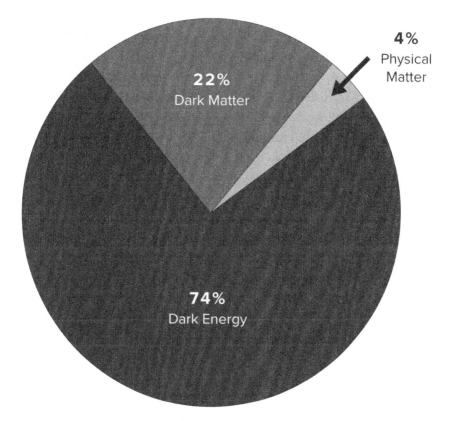

Figure 1: Science only knows 4% of all there is to know.

The most intelligent humans on the planet can understand and explain only 4% of what has been observed to be true; the rest of what is known is unexplainable. This does not even include aspects of truth or reality that we aren't even aware of yet. How many times have we assumed we knew the truth about a relationship we were entering into, been blindsided by things we didn't see coming, or been mistaken about how our life was going to turn out?

Science is based on proof through direct linear sequencing of cause and effect: "A" causes "B" causes "C." Scientific proof can be done through direct observation and validated through mathematic formulas and reproducibility. Science has created ways to increase observation both in the largest (cosmic) and smallest (quantum) perspectives through technology and advanced mathematical theory.

Medicine has advanced greatly in the treatment of acute diseases and conditions (such as the repair of bone fractures, blood or chemical imbalances, and treating infections) but has been woefully ineffective in curing chronic diseases. The advancements have been in the physical nature of diseases. If illnesses behaved in a linear fashion, then a certain treatment or surgical procedure would always be successful. We know, however, that that is not the case.

Like dark matter and dark energy, medicine doesn't know the causes and cures of many chronic illnesses such as autoimmune diseases, certain cancers, and painful conditions like fibromyalgia. Science can't even cure conditions as prevalent as essential hypertension or the common cold. Great scientific discoveries are made outside of convention. If what you are doing is not working, you have to think or do it differently. The answer may not reside in the obvious or the physical, but in the unseen or as-yet-unknown dimensions. Beyond the 4% is the place of creativity, mysticism, and the spirit. There are many stories of miraculous healings that are unexplainable. A miracle transcends the linear cause and effect of science. Miracles are phenomena that are observable and experiential, but because of the lack of an understandable connection, they are not provable. One has to surrender held beliefs of what is possible to enter the realm of the miracle.

The Ego

The most primitive level of consciousness with behavior involves reflex and instinct. This is commonly called the ego. The ego has existed as long as life has existed. On the most primitive level, the ego's purpose is for survival. It will compete with others to get what it wants: "survival of the fittest" and "kill or be killed." We all know a person who has a big ego. Many people identify themselves by their ego. The ego sees things as black and white. It is self-righteous and would rather die than be wrong. The ego is narcissistic and only thinks about what it wants. It seeks to control its environment and other people. It doesn't care how its actions affect others. The ego operates from the emotions of craving and fear. It desires what it can get from people and things. When it doesn't get what it wants or is given what it doesn't want, it lives in anger, grief, or fear. The ego lives in ignorance and can only see things one way. It doesn't know anything beyond itself and is afraid of what it doesn't know. Out of fear, the ego operates in denial and pretends things are not the way they truly are. It tries to resist what it sees as harmful. It is natural to not want to feel pain and emotional trauma. Denial is the ego's natural defense and conscious resistance to feeling. This leads to a mental block and resistance to feeling pain or suffering. In its most extreme forms, it can lead to amnesia—completely blocking out a traumatic event—but imbalance and disease remain because the feeling and memory remains below the conscious level, active in the subconscious like an infection. It is the primitive programming of life that keeps the human from its real *self*. It keeps a human from healing.

The Courage to Surrender

Ego is the obstacle to awareness and a higher potential of healing and of being. The more one tries to battle or resist the ego, the stronger it becomes. To be transcended, the ego must first be identified and understood. The individual has to be aware there is something greater than the self. The ego is similar to the 4% (in Figure 1) of all we think that exists, but there is a greater reality beyond our perceptions and beliefs. This is awareness and the place of miracles. Christians call this awareness divine, or Christ consciousness, and the Buddhists call it Buddha-nature. In Hindu tradition, it is *Jivatman*. When achieving greater awareness, the brain reroutes its neuropathways through the prefrontal lobe of the brain. Instead of self-absorption, there is a love and valuation of the relationship with another being as being more important. There is an expanded awareness and higher consciousness that leads to a different reality. This happens naturally to a woman when she gives birth. With the maternal-child bonding, the brain is rewired, and the narcissistic ego is transcended. With her child's birth, the mother's concern for her child is greater than her own needs and well-being. This is maternal instinct. With animals in nature, often we see a mother surrender her own life for the life of her child. The power of higher consciousness is beyond the ego and provides greater power. One hears stories of great feats of strength by a mother to save her child. In nature, a mother bear will attack a larger and stronger animal to save her cubs. A human mother will perform superhuman feats such as stopping a bus from running over her child or lifting a large object off her trapped child—an object that later takes several men to move. In men, the transition to a higher consciousness typically happens in warfare. A soldier will surrender his own life to save his band of brothers. Acts of courage and bravery lead him to overcome overwhelming odds in order to save his comrades or to accomplish a greater unifying mission.

Awareness is the transcendence beyond the ego of personal consciousness based on past experiences and judgments. Awareness is the opening of the mind to the realm of the possible. We increase our awareness with surrender. We surrender our old belief patterns of how we think things are and what they mean. Awareness through surrender is achieved through humility, courage, and perseverance. Humility is admitting we may not know the truth or what is real. The obstacles to greater awareness are fear and denial. It takes courage to overcome fear and admit one is wrong. Surrender is something that is counter to what the ego wants, but is the pathway of all spiritual practices. It is to give up what one is now in order to evolve into something greater. With the falling away of old beliefs, there is the fear of loss of identity—even if that identity created the illness or situation in the first place. Perseverance of intention supplies the energy that keeps one moving forward through all obstacles no matter what.

There are many examples of the power of surrender. Remember a time in your life when you were trying to remember a person's name or where you left your car keys? The harder you tried, the harder it was to remember. Only by surrendering and doing something else did the answer come. There are anecdotal stories of married couples trying to conceive a baby who gave up and adopted a baby. Later, with much less stress, they end up getting pregnant. Paradoxically, desiring something can make obtaining it more elusive. Stress occurs when we have unfulfilled expectations. When one surrenders those expectations, stress is released. One is able to see greater possibilities and opportunities. With greater awareness, one can see potentiality and have the ability to use it. One knows greater truth.

Unconscious Incompetence

There are four levels of consciousness in learning any new behavior. The lowest level is *unconscious incompetence*. It is based on ignorance. A person doesn't know how bad he is at something because he has never done it before. For example, a person has never driven a car before and doesn't know how difficult it is. The second lowest is *conscious incompetence*, in which one does the activity and realizes how incompetent he is. The third is *conscious competence*, in which a person has to concentrate on every aspect of the task (i.e., how much pressure to apply to the accelerator or brake, how much to turn the steering wheel, etc.). The highest level is *unconscious competence*, in which the activity becomes automatic, with minimal thought and great ease. In many cases, through repetition and development of habit, it is of great benefit to reach unconscious competence. One can perform the activity without thought. These habits are run in the subconscious. Operating from the subconscious is like operating on automatic pilot. At times, I have driven somewhere lost in thought and not realized how I got to my destination—or recalled any of the scenery I passed getting there. Our subconscious pilots our body and behavior based on experiences, routines, or habits. One doesn't have to consciously be aware of breathing or walking.

It may be assumed that the underlying activity of unconscious competence would be for one's highest benefit. The benefit is in not having to constantly relearn or focus on everything at all times. Habitual behaviors that were at one time thought to be beneficial or made us feel good, however, can become addictions. It takes reflection and contemplation of one's thoughts and actions to determine if those behaviors do serve the greater good. It is analogous to an experience that any golfer can attest to: trying to unlearn a previous pattern to develop a new way of swinging a golf club. It can be a painfully frustrating process, but in the end, the golfer is rewarded with higher achievement. In my exploration of the mind-body connection, I've had to unlearn much information about healing from my medical education that I previously presumed to be true. Albert Einstein once said, "The only thing that interferes with my learning is my education."

From Consciousness to Awareness

Albert Einstein hypothesized that we only use 10% of our brain. Some researchers believe that our consciousness utilizes only 1% of our brain. As we learn more, we realize how much we really don't know. If one was to know everything about everything humanity knows, we would still only know 4% of all there is to know. Our thoughts are mostly of events in the past or of the future—not what is happening in the present, where the rest of the brain exists on silent subconscious autopilot and in undiscovered unconsciousness. There are many unanswered questions involving creativity, imagination, and extrasensory phenomena such as remote viewing, remote healing, telepathy, telekinesis, intuition, and the commonalities of near-death experiences. These unexplainable phenomena are beyond the comprehension of the intellect and has historically been addressed by religious, philosophical, and spiritual contemplation. There is a vast amount of potential knowledge and power to be discovered.

Awareness comes from looking at a situation from more than one perspective. This is called abstraction. Abstraction and compassion are the same when used in relationships. They are the understanding of another's perceptions and perspective. The greater the number of understood and appreciated perspectives, the closer one arrives to the higher level of truth—and the greater the awareness. When in a conflict with another, one is able to gain a greater advantage by expanding one's awareness to understand the opponent's strengths, weaknesses, motivation, etc. Greater abstraction not only provides awareness on how an action may affect the immediate situation but also the consequences to others outside of the perceived sphere of influence. In other words, our actions have greater effect than what we imagined. Abstraction also takes into consideration what effect those actions might have over time. Thus, abstraction is the ability to extend awareness beyond personal space and time.

Great leaders were successful in being able to anticipate certain trends or conflicts by thinking outside themselves and putting themselves in other's shoes, looking at things from multiple and different perspectives. Getting many different perspectives from witnesses at a crime scene gives the investigative police officers a truer perspective of the event. In solving any problem, the more perspectives one takes into account from contrasting viewpoints, the greater the chance of arriving at the best course of action. Abraham Lincoln was secure enough to have political advisors of contrasting beliefs give him a greater understanding of any major issue. Gandhi would carefully study the perspectives, intentions, and habits of the representative from the British Empire to the point of mimicking the characteristics of the representative before meeting him for negotiations. In this way, Gandhi was able to gain a better understanding and a strategic advantage.

With increased consciousness and awareness, accidents and coincidence become replaced by synchronicity and serendipity. In awareness there are fewer accidents, because one is more conscious of his or her immediate surroundings. One is better able to identify the interconnectedness of otherwise seemingly irrelevant factors and become aware of the potential. Having this awareness, one is better able to anticipate an outcome and choose to either avoid or take advantage of it. With any conflict, being able to step back and try to understand the other's perspective leads to less anger and stress.

In summary, awareness is the open door we can walk through to change our lives. Our life as it is, is no longer working, and we want something different. As we have discussed throughout this chapter, we only know a small portion of what is real and true. We are held in our current situation by fear and ignorance. We tend to be more comfortable in known hells than unknown heavens. Awareness involves the courage to be open. It is about having the courage to surrender and say, "I really don't know what is real and what is not real anymore." It is an uncomfortable place to be. By being open to looking at things again from a different point of view, however, we can see the open door to the cage we are keeping ourselves in. Once we leave our cage, other doors of potential and possibility start to open that we were blinded to in the past. Our awareness starts with a better understanding of our thoughts and words.

Exercise

In the morning, noon, and evening for three days, repeat the following phrases: "I really don't know what is real and what is not real anymore," and "I am open to new possibilities."

CHAPTER FIVE

Thought and Word

"We are subject only to what we hold in mind."

—Sir David R. Hawkins, MD, PhD

"Change your thoughts and you change the world."

—Norman Vincent Peale

"The more man meditates upon good thoughts, the better will be his world and the world at large."

—Confucius

The brain contains 100 billion nerve cells called neurons. Each neuron is capable of generating a thought. Thought is the smallest component of consciousness. It is the root and foundation of who we think we are and what we represent. Thoughts are the building blocks of our personality and character.

Perception

Bits of sensory or perceptual information enter our brain through the sensory nerves. There are five sensory systems:

1.) vision or seeing,

2.) auditory or hearing,

3.) olfactory or smelling,

4.) gustatory or taste, and

5.) kinesthetic or feeling.

Earlier scientific research reportedly showed that there are over three million bits of sensory data that get relayed to the brain in any one instant. In vision, this may include the contours of objects, brightness or shadows, color, and contrast. In auditory, it may include the many sounds of background noise, tone, pitch, and volume. Tactilely or kinesthetically, we get input from the pressure of our body on the seat of the chair, our feet on the floor, the position of our joints in maintaining our posture, our hair brushing our face, the temperature of the room, the texture of the book, and/or our clothing against our body. In 1957, George Miller, a researcher in the study of consciousness, wrote a paper called "The Magical Number Seven, Plus or Minus Two," in which he claimed that the conscious mind is only able to focus on seven of the 3 million bits of sensory information. Some are only able to pay attention to five, while others are able to pay attention to nine bits of perceptual data. More recent research shows there are 20 million bits of sensory information that the brain gets exposed to every second, only forty of which enter a person's consciousness per second.

We may perceive the fragrance of a perfume or hear a nostalgic song that brings up memories of a first love. We may taste food that reminds us of a happy childhood dinner with family. Most of the perceptions, however, are never brought up into consciousness, though they are still stored in our memory.

Why is this important? Sometimes, these subconscious perceptions can trigger bodily responses that can affect our health. I went to a conference sponsored by University of California San Francisco and one of the lecturers, Dr. Linda Morse, was the director for the Kaiser Permanente occupational health program. Dr. Morse told of a patient who started a clerical job in an office and began experiencing migraine headaches. She missed some time from work on sick leave, then returned to work. After a time, the migraines returned. Again, she took time off work, but upon her return, her migraines also returned. Because she only had migraines at work, a worker's compensation claim was filed. The ergonomics of her chair and desk, along with lighting and ventilation, were assessed—and deemed non-factors to her illness. Dr. Morse was a sleuth and investigated in great depth. What the doctor discovered was that the woman's male supervisor wore the same aftershave as her step-father had worn when he was sexually abusing her as a child. Once this was brought to the woman's awareness, the migraines resolved. The woman had subconsciously remembered the smell, but because it wasn't on a conscious level, she hadn't been able to relate it to her childhood trauma.

Emotion, Thought, and Feeling

Thought always precedes form. The energy of the thought leads to action. Whether a house, a table, or a business, there is nothing that was not first a thought before it was created into form.

The brain controls the body. Thoughts are never neutral and are always charged with an emotion. Thoughts and the attached emotions can affect the healthy functioning of the body. Feelings in the body, like pain or warmth, can also lead to thoughts and emotions. Negative emotions (including shame, guilt, apathy, grief, fear, or anger) affect the functioning of the body. When you are angry, you can feel the muscles tighten and your heart rate quicken. Continuous negative thoughts and emotions causes stress, making these body changes more permanent and leading to disease. Positive emotions (including acceptance, love, and peace) lead to body changes that are beneficial, with greater power and healthier functioning.

It was thought that memories were filed chronologically or related to specific events. But research done by Gray and LaViolette in 1981 demonstrated that the memories are filed under *emotions*. There is a fear file, desire file, anger file, depression file, guilt file, etc. In each of the files, hundreds to several thousands of memories are stored. That is why, when a partner or family member triggers anger, the anger file is opened, and all the events that made you angry about that person come up—even events from the past related to other people. Events help feed the angry feeling. A single event opens a Pandora's box of anger, and a ripple is turned into a tsunami of anger. One's whole persona turns into anger that radiates and can be felt by others without speaking a word.

Science tells us that the average human thinks 16,000 thoughts a day. It has been estimated that 90% of thoughts are the same as the ones we had yesterday, and 80% of thoughts are negative (Cleveland Clinic: Wellness). Our thoughts are based on our memories of previous similar experiences. Emotions (such as anger, shame, and guilt) are attached to events of the past and the subsequent formation of belief. Anxiety and fear are related to the uncertainty of the future. Neither the past nor future exist in the present moment, and both are illusory. Not living in the present affects our view of the world. We have a tendency to hold onto those thoughts as if they were real and to see the world as scary or dangerous.

The mind doesn't want to feel emotional pain or fear. One of the tools the mind uses to avoid the pain of guilt and shame is *denial*. If I were to do something I perceived as wrong, I might change the story to rationalize and justify the action—or deny responsibility to avoid the fear of punishment. If I were in denial, I would still subconsciously know I was lying to myself. Even if the mind elects to keep the thought and feeling away from the conscious, that thought and feeling are still in the *subconscious* and affect the body's release of neurotransmitters and hormones that affect the body's functioning. Physical danger is temporary. Mental danger, however, can become permanent, leading to permanent chemical, electrical, energy-related, and ultimately, physical changes to the body that occur over time and create disease. Therefore, the body is a reflection of both conscious and subconscious thoughts held in the mind. It is the emotions we radiate that connect us with others. Words are used in an attempt to express our emotions or ideas.

Words

In the 3,000-year-old Hindu *Vedas*, sacred word was considered to be the primary creative force of the universe. In the King James Bible John 1:1 according to Saint John the Apostle, "In the beginning was the word. The word was with God and the word is God." Words are the expression of thoughts as symbols or labels that move energy from inside you out into the world. They are also used to share one's feelings or ideas with others. Words are able to inspire some or condemn others. Words have the power to move nations to greatness or toward destruction.

Water covers 70% of the Earth's surface. Interestingly, this is the same percentage of water that constitutes the human body. Water is the essential ingredient of life. Dr. Masaru Emoto conducted research into the measurement of wave fluctuations in water. He began taking photographs of frozen ice crystals. What he discovered was that water formed crystals unique to words expressing certain emotions placed on the water vessel. He photographed the crystal formations of ice after being exposed to positive words (such as love, beauty, and gratitude) and negative (such as hate, vulgarity, and condemnation). Amazingly, the crystals of the positive affirmations were of great beauty, whereas the negative affirmations did not produce crystals or produced crystals that were grotesque. If words can have such profound affect on something as seemingly inanimate as water, one must consider the power our words have on ourselves and on life.

Words are not the same as thoughts. The same word may have different meanings based on personal experience. We may think of one word for snow, whereas an Inuit may have a hundred discerning words for snow that are essential for his survival. If you've ever gotten into an argument with a loved one over the misinterpretation of words or events, you know that no two people look at the world the same way. Your spouse's idea of the word *love* may be totally different from your own.

How often do we use words without realizing their true power? How often do we use negative words such as *stop*, *don't*, and *can't*? We tell our children, "Don't play in the street," or, "Stop making a mess."

Try this experiment: Whatever you do for the next thirty seconds, don't think of the Statue of Liberty. Stop thinking of the Statue of Liberty.

Now, what did you think of? Almost all people will think of the Statue of Liberty. The *don't* or *stop* words get our attention, and we remember the rest of the statement. What we may actually be telling our kids is to play in the street and to make a mess.

When we hold something in mind, we focus on that thought, whether positive or negative. When meeting my pain patients for the first time, I ask them what they want, and they always say, "To not have pain." What they are doing, however, is focusing on their pain and putting their intention on their pain. We tell ourselves or others, "Don't be depressed," "Don't get angry," or, "Stop thinking about that!" We are reinforcing the thought or activity, however, that we want to change or stop.

Instead of thinking in negatives and using words like *stop*, *don't*, or *can't*, think of how you would rather be. For example, instead of thinking, "Don't be depressed," think of how you would rather be. If you would rather be happy, just think, "I'm going to be happy." Instead of "Don't be so angry," think, "How can I look at things differently to find humor in this situation?"

How often do we use powerless words like *hope*, *wish*, or *try*? What if I said, "I'll try to make it to your party," or "I hope to make it to your party," or "I wish I could make it to your party?" Using the words *hope*, *wish*, or *try* leaves an uncertainty or lack of commitment. These are words of weakness of action, instead of a word like *will*.

Webster's Dictionary defines the word *will* as "the power of choice or control over one's own action toward a strong, fixed purpose." Feel the different energy of saying, "I will make it to your party." *Will* is a word of confidence and conviction. It gives a powerful focus to the mind that also energizes the body.

We all have inner critics that tell us things that are hurtful. If someone else were to tell us the same things, we would want to kill him. We accept what the inner critic tells us as defining who we are. Don Miguel Ruiz wrote the book *The Four Agreements*, which is derived from Mesoamerican Toltec teachings to help bring a person more into his spiritual self and lead a richer, fuller life. The first agreement is to "Be impeccable with your word." It is considered not only the most important but also the most difficult to maintain and honor. The word *impeccable* means "without sin," and the sin begins with the rejection of the self. The original definition of the word *sin* was "in error" or "in ignorance." Ignorance is seen as the root of sin in Buddhism, Hinduism, and Christianity. The three poisons in Buddhism are attachment (desire), ignorance, and hatred. Ignorance is the original sin as depicted in the Bible's book of Genesis. Out of ignorance, Eve ate the apple in the Garden of Eden.

The words we use are the most powerful tool we have as humans. They can, however, be a double-edged sword. Our words can bring us increased happiness and peace, but they can also lead to destruction and the death of relationships. Once said, words cannot be taken back. We often tell ourselves, "I'm too fat," "I'm too stupid," "I don't deserve it," or "I can't do anything right." Words can be like a thought virus that can infect other's minds. We can tell our children, "You're good for nothing, just like your father," "You're not good enough," or "You drive me crazy." The inner critic is poison not only to the other person but also to the *relationship* with that other person. The virus can also spread and poison the community through gossip. Gossip is used to demean or tear down others so a person can feel better about himself or herself. Gossip poisons the relationships of all the people in the community.

To be impeccable in our speech also means to honor our word as truth. Truth and positive thought are supportive to life and relationships. Speaking in truth is a sign of respect for a relationship with oneself and others. We make promises to others in the moment that we have no intention in keeping. We lie to protect ourselves or to keep from being perceived as bad. We think it is harmless, but it has a powerful affect on trust in a relationship. The Native Americans used to talk of the white man's "forked tongue" as a lie to get what he wanted.

Words are an expression of meaning to the individual and are used to give meaning to perceptions. For example, a feeling in the stomach might be interpreted as the word *hunger*. This leads to the desire for food and the act of eating. Words as labels can be associated with other words. When one is told one has diabetes, a cascade of associated emotions of fear and anger can permeate a person. Diabetes may trigger other words like *weakness, illness, debilitation, medicine,* and *injections,* along with terms like *kidney and nerve damage* and *early death.* The problem is that what we hold in mind tends to manifest. If we think all these things will happen, they will happen. Our minds play a major role in creating the disease and the consequences. We become victims and give away our power to the word and to the disease. This can be true for any condition or disease.

As we have mentioned, a feeling energy arises, and we put a label on it. By labeling a feeling with a word, it changes the body's physiology and leads to a course of action. When we label an arising inner energy as *hunger, anger,* or *pain,* we have to control and act upon it. These words are interpreted by the mind as negative. We want to fight or resist the feeling. Various negative emotions affect brain chemistry that releases hormones, activates the sympathetic nervous system, and blocks acupuncture systems that affect the body, impair healing, and cause disease. Pain or disease may arise in the body, but it is the thoughts and negative emotions that cause debility and disability. If we are able to have a positive attitude about the symptom, we give the body the maximum benefit in healing.

One has to separate the feeling from the thought and word. One has the feeling of an aching stomach, muscle tension, or a sinking feeling—without labeling it as *hunger, anger,* or *despair.* Labeling the feeling with a word leads to a certain action, such as eating when hungry, attacking when angry, or becoming paralyzed when afraid. Feelings don't go on forever. They tend to arise, crest, and dissipate like a wave. One can hold onto the feeling with self-righteousness. Thought and word perpetuates the feeling by justifying it, instead of allowing the feeling to arise and dissolve or fall away.

Scientific research has shown that what we think about tends to manifest. When we put emotion such as fear and worry into something in the future that we don't want, it is more likely to happen. With a thought that one doesn't want, put no emotion or energy into it, and it will gradually disappear. Visualizing something one wishes to manifest with devotion and holding the feeling of having received or accomplished it, will greatly increase the power to change potentiality to reality. That's how miracles are created. It is about setting the intention and eliminating the emotional attachment. It is realizing that holding onto a feeling is a choice.

Thought manifests into word,

Word manifests into deed,

Deed develops into habit,

And habit hardens into character.

So watch your thoughts and its ways with care,

Born out of care for all sentient beings,

For as the shadow follows the body,

As you think so you become.

Buddha

Exercises

1. Eliminate the negative self-talk. Practice saying what you do want instead of what you don't want. Instead of saying, "I don't want pain," or "I don't want to be fat," speak in the positive. Picture in your mind how you want to be. What would you rather be doing? How would you rather feel about yourself?

2. Eliminate words or labels. Discern that there is a difference between feelings and emotions. Words define the emotion. When we label something as *anger, fear, sadness, pain* or *hunger*, we become that word. The natural tendency is to resist the emotion and the feeling, but that just reinforces the reaction and makes it stronger. Just release the thought and focus on the body's reaction to the thought or the breath: "Oh, I notice my muscles are tightening, and my breath is getting more shallow." Do not try to change anything, but allow it to be as it is. If you truly let go, then after a few minutes, it will be gone.

3. What you resist persists. What you desire moves away from you. You naturally want to resist any emotion that causes pain. This is true for any emotion. Take, for example, if you are afraid or worried. By resisting the emotion, it persists and gets stronger. As my teacher, David Hawkins, would tell his students who suffered from anxiety and worry, "The problem with you is you don't worry

enough." You need to worry or be afraid *more*. You need to allow yourself to get all the worry out of your mind and body. By devoting practice to this technique, the emotional reaction will be greatly reduced or gone.

4.   Don't speak ill of others. Gossip is poison not only for others but for you as well.

CHAPTER SIX

Truth

"Men occasionally stumble over the truth, but most of them pick themselves up and hurry off as if nothing ever happened."

—Sir Winston Churchill

"The fact that a great many people believe something is no guarantee of its truth."

—W. Somerset Maugham, The Razor's Edge

"There is no god higher than truth."

—Mahatma Gandhi

"Ye shall know the truth, and the truth shall make you free."

—The Holy Bible, John 8:32

As a father, I found parenting one of the most rewarding and challenging experiences of my life. At times, I discovered more about myself than I really wanted to admit. It was a true epiphany that the characteristics in my son that drove me the craziest were characteristics I had in myself that I refused to acknowledge. It was truly a humbling and yet enlightening experience. Several years ago, I had a discussion with my teenage son who had the belief that reality was "whatever I wanted it to be." This debate occurred as a result of his justification of his behaviors as a teenager that conflicted with my parental judgment. He felt that each individual had an independent personal view of reality based on his or her personal experience and interpretation. He reasoned that each person's point of view was correct, which was similar to Karl Marx's philosophy of relative truth. This is true on one level. We tend to base our reality on the judgments of our experiences. In this case, my son's truth did not agree with my truth. Relative truth is self-righteous truth. Wars are waged based on whose truth is more "right."

Is there such a thing as a higher truth beyond one's personal, subjective truth? Some would consider a higher truth or reality as one that has the consensus of the greatest number of people. This, however, would not explain how certain historical "truths" were later proven to be false. The realities, such as the world being flat or the sun revolving around the Earth, were later debunked by the evolution of science and discovery. Many erroneous beliefs were defended by religion and rulers who benefited from maintaining certain beliefs. Galileo wasn't officially exonerated by the Catholic Church until the 1980s for his proclamation that the earth rotated around the sun. Science, itself, is limited in its truth and is based on perception, politics, and erroneous theories, which are later brought to light. Science has attempted to increase its ability to perceive both on the macro (astronomic) and micro (quantum) realms and has used advanced mathematics to expand knowledge beyond the perceivable.

I asked my son if his subjective truth was the ultimate truth, which would mean that what he believed as a five-year-old was the same truth he would have as a teenager or adult. I look back in my life about decisions and actions I made when I was younger and admit my ignorance. Through the experiences I have had in my life, I tend to look at things differently. When I allow myself to gain a different perspective, I gain awareness and wisdom. Personal truth is based on experience and interpretation of that experience. If my reality is truth, then what if it conflicts with another person's truth? By changing perspective and looking at the situation through another's eyes or by "walking in their shoes," I may discover a higher truth that I was guilty of unknowingly contributing to the conflict.. Greater truth comes from compassion—by seeing things from a different perspective than one's own experience.

Energy is required for life to think and to act. Whether one is trying to learn something new or simply go out for a jog, energy is expended and flows through the entire body. Science tells us there is an energy flow from the body to the brain providing information, then brain energy flows back down to the organs and muscles in response. As mentioned in the chapter on thought, all thoughts are attached to emotions. Diseases in organs can cause imbalances of energetic flow that can cause weakness in muscles. The imbalance of life energetic flow can also cause disease in organs. Western science knows of the energetic connectedness between the brain and muscles. When part of the brain gets damaged from a stroke, disrupted energetic pathways can affect the sensation or muscle strength of the corresponding part of the body. Abnormal thoughts or living in lies can affect muscles and organs, as well. An example of this is the use of polygraph tests to measure physiologic responses to untruths. Lies affect the heart, lungs, and electrical conductivity of the skin. The mind can tell lies, but the body knows the truth. How does this work?

Denial

As mentioned in the previous chapter, the mind uses denial for perceived survival and to escape suffering. A lie is a denial of truth and is created by the mind to block physical or emotional pain from conscious awareness. Negative emotions and denial take much more brain energy, which depletes energy from the rest of the body. The location of the blockage of that neural connection in the brain can affect organs and muscles that are also energetically connected.

People live in lies because of shame, guilt, fear, desire, anger, or pride. It often starts in childhood, when a child fears punishment for telling the truth. To avoid punishment, lies are told as a means of self-protection and safety. Sometimes, we are taught by our parents not to honor our feelings; other times, when physical or emotional pain becomes too severe, we stop feeling, and the interconnection of the mind with the body is resisted and disconnected. At times, we learn to not honor our own feelings. Shame always comes from the beliefs outside oneself. Beliefs come from the rules of the family or community that may or may not be true. Giving power (energy) to others takes energy away from you. Accepting the condemnation of others in shame, guilt, or fear leaves you weak and affects your health. Dr. David Hawkins says that all diseases come from unconscious guilt. Guilt is tied to anger and fear. When you become angry with another person, unconsciously there is guilt. If you take action against the other person out of anger, you fear possible retaliation or revenge. Guilt gives other's opinions or beliefs power over yours. When you go against yourself, you try to destroy yourself by creating autoimmune diseases. To prevent this self-punishment, you may deny anything happened or deny anything is wrong. The truth, however, is still in the subconscious and can cause harm to the body. The subconscious controls much of the body's functions. Lies and denial work on the conscious level but don't work on the subconscious level. Expanding oneself with anger or pride makes us look more imposing to an opponent. This self-expansion, however, consumes a larger amount of the body's energy and cannot be maintained indefinitely. Expanding oneself in pride tends to fortify self-importance and self-righteousness, which makes it more difficult to transcend the ego to greater awareness and truth.

Being able to discern truth enables a person to know what is supportive of life and what is not. Nothing that is a lie is supportive of life, because, obviously, it doesn't really exist. A child can't pretend he can fly and successfully jump off the roof of a house. A person can't survive on imaginary water or food.

As one's level of consciousness evolves, beliefs and truths change. At the lowest levels, truth is about survival. Truth is self-serving: kill or be killed; survival of the fittest; or "what's in it for me?" What serves the self is thought to be the greatest good. We see that individuals, companies, and governments that live by that credo remain in poverty and are unsustainable.

Loyalty vs. Integrity

Loyalty comes from a feeling of specialness in belonging. Loyalty can relate to family, friends, work, a sports team, a community, a country, or religion. Loyalty is a very admirable characteristic because it builds trust, a sense of belonging, and interconnectedness. It is what connects us by values and sets rules of behavior for the protection of self and others. One can't just decide to disobey traffic lights at a busy intersection or disrespect the rights of others by taking their possessions.

Paradoxically, loyalty also can have a dark side. Nepotism, cronyism, partisanship, and prejudice lack integrity. The criminal element survives out of loyalty based in fear and intimidation. Instead of hiring the most qualified candidate, one can hire or give business to another who is a friend or family member or of the same race or religion—despite lesser qualifications. Fairness is relative and based on whether one benefits or is excluded from opportunity.

Out of loyalty, the individual is subject to the rules of the group. One is also given a role in the community that identifies how one fits in to the relationship with other members. There may be some sort of abuse: sexual, physical, mental, or abuse through neglect. The rules of the community play a large role in how the individual views himself or herself. A family or community may wish to maintain status quo and choose to ignore injury to the individual. This can occur when the perpetrator is in a position of power. The individual is then told that his or her perception of events and reality is wrong. Loyalty can also lead to guilt and shame. Does the individual honor his or her own feelings or surrender to the "truth" of others? Abuse to the individual may be held as a secret of the family or community because of pride or shame.

Science has proven that disease is caused by stress. Stress can be caused by an inner conflict between what one desires and what is acceptable based on the rules of the family or community. It can be a conflict between loyalties versus personal integrity. Loyalty can be used to block the truth. Out of loyalty or obligation, we may do things based on guilt. To maintain relationships with our parents, spouse, children, or friends, we may compromise ourselves and surrender our better judgment and energy to them. There is no greater unconditional love than a mother has for her child. That love, however, can blind a mother from the reality of the true nature of her child. The mother's love of the Sandy Hook Elementary School shooter, Adam Lanza, prevented her from seeing the danger her son presented to herself and others. The 2013 Boston Marathon bombing suspects' mother still feels her sons are good boys and are innocent. Out of ego, mothers feel their children can do no wrong and are better than they truly are. This belief is not grounded in truth, compassion, or concern for others.

Loyalty can be based in love or based in fear. When loyalty is based in love, there is no conflict. When loyalty is based in fear or untruths, there is the stress of conflict. You can tell when you act out of love or gratitude. You can feel the energy and power within you—and within the recipient of the act. When you do an activity that you really don't want to do, go to a job you hate, or visit a person you dislike, you can feel the energy drain out of you. When acting out of obligation, you feel the energy drain out of you while performing the act. The energy drain is your life energy being given to someone else. Living in obligation leads to inner conflict and disease.

Truth Is Reality

How often do we wish our lives were different? We can fall into anger or blame when we don't get what we want. Sometimes, we are given something we don't want or not given something we *do* want. We can feel sorry for ourselves and feel we deserve things to be different.

Truth is reality, and reality is truth. What you have, you have, and what you don't have, you don't have. In large part, you are where you are because of the decisions you have made and the actions you have taken in the past. Your actions may have seemed like the truth. What you thought was a good idea at the time may not have worked out, but the truth always prevails in consequence. You only have control over what you have control over. You do not have any control over what other people may say or do. You have limited control over whether a child or parent wants a relationship with you. You only have control over yourself. To want some different reality beyond your control causes stress and affects your sense of well-being.

Truth Is Power

The universe operates in perfect balance between worlds of form (physical) and non-form (the unmanifest or potential energy). Water serves as an example of this principle. Out of the vastness of the ocean, when conditions are right, an iceberg will form. At other times, the ocean water evaporates to form clouds and rain. Even though water is in different forms—solid (iceberg), liquid (water), or gas (clouds)—it is still water. As with water changing forms, energy changes to matter, and matter changes to energy. This is the scientific first law of thermodynamics. It states that there is a balance between matter and energy, the two of which make up all that we know exists. Transforming matter requires energy. Transforming trees, metal, and other materials in order to build a house requires energy. Like the energy released by burning a log, matter starts to disintegrate, releasing the energy that was used to create it. This released energy returns to the pool of energy potential. Physics tells us that the universal tendency is toward simplicity or non-form. There is energy involved in creation. The more complex the form, the more energy required to create and maintain it. When energy is withdrawn from maintaining the physical form, it will start to deteriorate.

Lies are the most complex creations, because they are not real. Lies are inventions of the mind, without substance or the ability to become real outside of the mind. It takes much energy to maintain a lie. A person who lives in lies and builds his or her reality through lies soon cannot tell the difference between a truth and a lie. The more one lies, the more energy it takes to maintain one's illusion of reality, and the weaker one becomes. The body accommodates thought and becomes what one perceives or thinks of as the truth. One becomes the lie or the illusion. In some ways, we are like Pinocchio: When we live in denial or lies, our body changes to form disease. Pinocchio wanted to become a real boy and had to learn to tell the truth. Truth enhances and supports life. Truth is more energy efficient and provides better balance and greater awareness. The mind can lie, but the body always tells the truth. One needs to live in truth to find one's genuine self to heal and become whole.

The truth is that you aren't responsible for another's emotions or actions, which is a powerful truth. All we can do is treat others the way we would like to be treated. Sometimes, we unintentionally cause others to interpret our actions as insults. Another person's anger, criticism, or blame are not yours—unless you agree to accept them. Truth is totally under your control and is based on choice. Guilt and shame are illusions based on the judgments of others in an attempt to control you.

The lies we tell ourselves of things we think are essential oftentimes aren't essential at all. The truth is that the things we think will make us happy only provide short-term satisfaction and breed fear, because what is outside ourselves can always be taken away—whether it be money, a house, a loved one, or a career.

Living in truth brings great power, because truth is supportive of life, and falsehood is not. That which is false has no power, because it is not real. Realities based on lies have no substance and eventually fail. Living in truth is never easy. Often, we tell "white lies" to protect the feelings and beliefs of loved ones or to protect ourselves. In truth, most people don't want to know the truth. Most of the time, lies are maintained out of fear. Lies tend to create other lies that are then used to support and rationalize the original lies, which become a person's reality. Being truthful means living with accountability and self-respect. Living with integrity honors self-worth and personal responsibility. Being personally responsible for your thoughts, words, and actions leads to greater personal power and happiness.

Truth and Love

Is there a difference between love and compassion? Love is a subjective quality that means different things to different people. There are different facets and levels of love. The lowest level that some describe as love is the same as lust or desire. This love is believed to be external and comes from outside oneself. It is about possessing someone like a thing or property. Oftentimes, with this level of love, there is fear of loss and the desire to control the other person. No one likes to be controlled, and instead of bringing people closer together, it drives relationships apart. External love can also be about the love of "desiring." It is not about loving the other person but about winning and owning the other person. Once what was desired is obtained, it may give temporary satisfaction or happiness, but there will always be something else to be desired. External love can be about engendering envy from others. In relationships based on desiring, the partner is like a trophy that feeds off the desire and envy from others. The greater the desire and envy engendered from others, the greater one's own primitive level of self-esteem.

Another aspect of primitive love is giving to the other what you want them to have instead of what they really want. For example, a husband buying a nice, sexy dress for his wife that is too small because he wants her to lose weight. That won't go over very well with her. Or imagine your mother-in-law doing or saying something that she thinks is in your best interest, but that you interpret as criticism. The situation can play out between parents and spouses, as well. A loving relationship ends, and feelings are changed about the other person.

Another type of love is romantic love. Romantic love comes from a mental picture of the perfect relationship—of just seeing the good or how things *should* be. At this level of love, we expect the other to meet all our expectations and make us happy. This is an impossible task, however, and can never be fulfilled. Sometimes, a person in romantic love believes that love can overcome obstacles that affect the relationship: "My love will change him." No one can change another person, however, unless that other person wants to change. Loving in expectation of a different outcome causes personal suffering. We have to accept the situation with another the way it is at present.

Some say love is blind (i.e., that we blindly trust in the goodness of another without knowing his or her true intention). This occurs during the initial passion phase of a relationship but can continue throughout the entirety of a relationship until the truth is revealed. In romantic love, there is a denial of the other's truth. Seeing the world with rose-colored glasses is seeing the good in someone without seeing his or her lack of integrity. Relationships are started out of love, but more than half the time, they end in breakup. This can lead to disillusionment. Few things can be as devastating as the betrayal of faith and trust. There is no truth in the belief that if you are nice to someone, they will be nice to you. There is no truth in the belief that everyone shares the same values and beliefs. My teacher David Hawkins stated more than half the people in the US don't come from a position of integrity and are "wolves in sheep's clothing." We all know people we thought were loved ones, only to find out later they misrepresented themselves to fulfill their own self-serving intentions. Socrates said man always does what he thinks is for the good. For some, the greatest good is what is best for *them* and not necessarily for you.

Sometimes, out of low self-esteem, we think that love is a sacrifice of personal truth to satisfy the needs of the other in the relationship. The relationship, however, shouldn't be harmful to us. As mentioned earlier, there can be a fear or guilt that keeps us in a harmful relationship. In truth, living in fear or guilt is not love or compassion; it is ignorance and lack of truth that is the problem. The problem is that one doesn't see the lack of integrity in oneself. If one lived in truth, there would be no blind side, and one could discern the falsity in another.

There is a patient I treated whom I call "The Postman." He was a sixty-two-year-old male who had injured his lower back on the job more than six months before I saw him. He had originally injured himself while delivering mail on a Saturday by climbing into the mail vehicle and twisting to throw his mail satchel into the backseat. He had had all the appropriate radiologic testing and treatment with physical therapy but had not gotten any better. When I saw him, he was still not working and was in pain. I examined him and diagnosed him with piriformis syndrome, which is an injury to a muscle that attaches the hip to the sacrum. I would have treated him ten years before by explaining the diagnosis, keeping him off work, and treating him with pain killers, muscle relaxants, and anti-inflammatories, then sending him for physical therapy. When I saw him, however, with what I had learned, I treated him differently. In a more holistic approach, I asked him more questions to gather more information about his soul. He informed me that he had been working for the Postal Service for more than forty years. Originally, the job was helpful in helping him pay his way through college, but he had never intended to work for the Postal Service for so long. He had a wife at home who wanted him to keep working because it generated more income, and he had two adult daughters in their twenties living at home whom he was helping to support. We kept talking, and suddenly, he started crying and said, "I've just had a revelation. I've just had an epiphany. I'm sixty-two years old, and what I wanted to do all my life—and the reason I went to school—was to become a writer. I know what I need to do now. Let's close this injury claim. I need to move on with my life."

I never saw him again, but I know his life was not the same after our visit. I gave him the awareness that his back pain was not the real issue; the real issue was that he subconsciously didn't want to keep working, and he was living his life for everyone else but himself. I addressed his compromised spirit, which was the root of his disease. He was working out of loyalty and obligation to others, rather than honoring himself. By bringing into awareness his suppressed desires, it gave him permission to follow his bliss. That was more gratifying to me than to just treat his symptoms. It was not only a gift for him but for me, as well. It helped me realize that true healing oftentimes means transcending the linear concepts of traditional medicine. As a healer, one must look into the heart of the other to perceive the lies or defective programs they are running that are causing their disease.

The highest level of love is that of unconditional love. Spiritual teacher Adyashanti says that a truly loving relationship is accepting the other the way they are and not trying to change them. Love is about surrendering oneself for the relationship. It is seeing the oneness of all life. It is seeing another as just as important as yourself and seeing yourself as important as another. Another person's child is just as valuable as your own child. The truth of this level of love has great power. It is at this level that miracles and healing start to happen.

Truth Is Compassion

What is compassion? Compassion is the ability to see from another's perspective. What if I were a police detective and wanted to find out what happened at a crime scene? I would not only ask for the details of the event from the victim but might also interview the perpetrator for a motive. I might also get perspective of any witnesses. The more points of view I get about the event, the better I would be able to find the truth.

There is a story about four blind men and an elephant. One felt the tusk and thought the elephant was a spear. The second felt the trunk and thought the elephant was a snake. The third felt the ear and thought the elephant was a fan. The fourth blind man felt the body and thought the elephant was a rug. Each, with his limited perception, was correct but was nevertheless incorrect.

Only by combining their individual perspectives into one perspective would the blind men get a truer picture of reality.

My teacher David Hawkins said that compassion is being able to look into another's heart for the truth without judgment. No one sees the world in exactly the same way. My view of the world is based on my experience. The obstacle to truth is when someone thinks that his or her perspective is the only true reality.

As with love, there are different levels of compassion. The lowest level of compassion is pity and mercy. This is the beginning of forgiveness. You can forgive someone without loving them. Forgiveness comes from understanding another's perspective outside your own. The highest level of compassion is greater than personal love; the highest compassion involves love and discernment. Discernment is seeing another person in his or her entirety. Some call it the Buddhist "third eye." The truth of compassion cuts through the blind side of personal love. Al-Anon is an organization that assists the loved ones and family of addicts. In order to help the addict, compassion is required more than love. Instead of giving into whatever the addict wants, the greater good and the more compassionate action would be allowing the addict to fail. In the highest level of compassion, decisions are made that are not only best for the loved one but for all of humanity.

So, compassion has a wide range. Compassion is caring without attachment. It is in seeing the sameness of all beings. Compassion is not seeing one more special or important than another. At its highest level, compassion, unconditional love and truth become one.

To live in compassion is to live in truth. In truth, as one develops more compassion for others, one develops more compassion for oneself, and as one develops more compassion for oneself, one develops more compassion for others. Compassion comes from humility and forgiveness. You can't give what you don't have. You can't give food unless you have food to give. You can't give money if you have no money. You can't see truth until you live in truth. You can't have love unless you know what love is and have love for yourself. By having love, you become love and are able to give love.

What I have discovered in studying different healing practices, as well as different religious practices, is the commonality in the practices of the higher truth. The highest truth is universal. Spiritually, God is omniscient, able to understand from an infinite number of perspectives, and therefore, of ultimate truth.

Defining Highest Truth

What are the characteristics of the highest truth? Truth is universal to all people and has reverence for all life. It is timeless and applicable to any time in the past or future. Truth is not based on any emotion except compassion. It is nonjudgmental and non-controlling. Truth is inspirational and influences us toward self-empowerment and happiness.

Truth is supportive of life and happiness. With higher truth, we are able to strip away values and beliefs that keep us from living a full and healthy life. We no longer operate thought programs that may cause suffering and disease. By surrendering to higher truth, we are able to expand our awareness to see new opportunities for our lives that were previously hidden and that we didn't think were possible.

So how does one learn compassion? Compassion is developed through forgiveness.

Exercises:

1. Speak and live in truth. Honor yourself and others by honoring and committing to your word. That which is a lie or illusory is not supportive of your life or your relationships. Supporting lies takes energy from you and can cause disease. Living in truth breaks down denial and leads to courage.

2. Feel your body for the truth. Living in lies, whether out of loyalty or obligation, drains energy meant for health.

3. Respect your own needs. List one or two things you can do for yourself every day. By nourishing yourself, you are better able to give to others.

4. Be compassionate toward others. Realize that acting out of love and acceptance is more for your own well-being than for the well-being of others.

CHAPTER SEVEN

Forgiveness

"When you hold resentment toward another, you are bound to that person or condition by an emotional link that is stronger than steel. Forgiveness is the only way to dissolve that link and get free."

—Catherine Ponder

"For if ye forgive men their trespasses, your heavenly Father will also forgive you: But if ye forgive not men their trespasses, neither will your Father forgive your trespasses."

—The Holy Bible: Matthew 6:14–15

"Resentment is like drinking poison and waiting for the other person to die."

—source unknown

"The weak can never forgive. Forgiveness is the attribute of the strong."

—Mahatma Gandhi

My father passed away shortly after I made the decision to leave my job after twenty-on years, and my mother's health was breaking down. She ended up having four major surgeries over a year and a half. I sold my house and moved in with her to provide myself some respite from the "rat race" and to offer her some assistance while she convalesced following my father's death and her surgeries. It was a bit of an adjustment for both of us.

My mother likes to collect clocks with various chimes and alarms—despite the fact that she had gotten hard of hearing. She would turn the volume of the clocks to their loudest setting and still not hear the chimes or alarms. The clocks would have musical tunes, rooster crows, chimes, gongs, and announced time blaring, "The time is now 3 a.m.!" The chimes would sound every hour all night. My mother also wanted to start getting up early, so she would set her alarm clock for 6 a.m. and turn the volume up loud. Because she couldn't hear it, however, the alarm would continuously sound from 6 a.m. to 10 a.m., when she would finally wake up. I learned to keep my bedroom door closed at night.

I had been in private practice for twenty-one years, had been the medical director of a specialty hospital for twenty years, and at times, had had to make critical decisions regarding patient medical care. My mother pointed out, however, that I didn't know how to do my laundry right or how to put the dishes in the dishwasher correctly. To my mother, I was twelve years old again and had not learned anything since that time.

At times, I felt anger, as old buttons were pushed in my perception of my mother's disrespect for me. After much reflection, however, I realized that I was reacting as if I were twelve and that when she would "push my buttons," it was actually *me* pushing my own emotional buttons. I had to laugh to myself at the drama I had created and carried with me all my life. Reflecting and recontextualizing provided me with the perfect opportunity to resolve my old issues. In the end, we got along as well as we ever had and became the best of friends, for which I will always be grateful.

Forgiveness is the most powerful pillar of healing. In the years we conducted study groups for the patients in the clinic, the lesson on forgiveness had the greatest impact on people's lives. It is the foundation of Christianity: Jesus came into the world for mankind's salvation, and salvation comes from forgiveness. In the King James Bible, Luke 23:34 at the time of his crucifixion, Jesus said, "Father, forgive them, for they know not what they do."

We all have had the experience of getting angry or upset when not getting what we want or when others don't act the way we feel they should. Resentment can also come from feeling wronged by life or God. Often, it is the person closest to us who hurts us the most: a best friend, a parent, a spouse, a sibling, or a child. The greater the trust, the more vulnerable and angry we feel when betrayed. They know which emotional buttons to push. There is a sense of injustice and self-righteousness. I think, "I'm right, and everyone else is wrong. They don't play by the same rules of moral decency that I feel all people should live by." The truth is we can't enforce our rules on anyone else. Whenever we have expectations of how other people should act, we get disappointed. Resentment occurs when others don't live up to our expectations. Maybe they are just doing the best job they can do.

Resentment is holding onto the feelings of anger for long periods of time, even lifetimes. Often, the resentment transcends the actual event and is identified with the persons involved. Every time you see that person, resentment and anger resurface. The other person may or may not even be aware of the resentment. Sometimes, the resentment is held even after the perpetrator has died. With resentment, the anger may become part of your identity. Holding onto anger hurts you much more than it hurts the perceived perpetrator. It gives the other person control over your emotional well-being.

Forgiveness is an escape from living a life of fear or anger. We blame others, or we blame life for the way things are. Anger makes one view the world and everyone else with anger. What underlies anger is fear, weakness, and a sense of helplessness. Sometimes, we use anger to feel more powerful and in control. We can use anger to justify the manipulation and control of others. Sometimes, we use anger to provide a sense of safety and protection. The truth is, anger makes us a victim. By being a victim, we don't take responsibility for our feelings or events in our lives. Sometimes, we are unwilling to forgive because of fear. Something happened that was so hurtful, we won't forgive, because we don't want to be hurt again. Sometimes, we don't forgive out of pride. Pride is the belief that we are right, and everyone else is wrong. Pride is the unwillingness to look at anyone else's point of view. Like anger, pride is a defense mechanism for underlying fear and ignorance. Sometimes, we live in guilt for something that we did and feel was wrong. We beat ourselves up and feel we are unworthy or undeserving of love and compassion.

What Is Forgiveness?

Imagine there is a giant hook with a sharp barb on the end that is going through your body and causing you great pain. Also on the hook, just outside of you, is the person who wronged you. You want to get off the hook and don't want that person next to you, but you are both hooked together. The only way to release yourself is by letting the other person off the hook first, which then releases you. This is forgiveness.

Forgiveness is not about forgetting or denying a hurtful event that took place, condoning the event, or reconciling with the offender. It is not repressing hurt feelings by pretending everything is fine when it isn't. Forgiveness is not for the benefit of the perpetrator, but for the health and well-being of the self. Forgiveness can take many forms. It may look like reconciliation, or it may look like completely cutting off the relationship with the other person.

Forgiveness is letting oneself off the hook. By not forgiving, we are tied to the other person for the rest of our life. It is ironic that by not forgiving, we give the other person power over our mind and body. We think that by holding onto our hurt, it will hurt the other person, when we are really only hurting ourselves. As the above quote says, "Resentment is like drinking poison and waiting for the other person to die."

Oscar Wilde said, "Always forgive your enemies. Nothing annoys them so much." Forgiveness is about personal power. A life well lived is your greatest revenge. Focusing on your wounded feelings gives the person who caused the pain power over you. Live with beauty, kindness, and love.

Forgiveness is about taking back your life. Forgiveness involves the dismantling of the way we look at hurtful events. It is not just saying, "I forgive you," or, "I forgive myself." It is not done only with the brain but also with the heart. I can say, "I forgive you," while I grit my teeth and flare my nostrils, but this is not forgiveness. Forgiveness may start with the brain in making a conscious effort to want to see things differently. It then evolves, and through the heart, it gets incorporated into the body to allow healing.

The Physiology of Forgiveness

The mind stores memories and beliefs that direct the way the body interacts with its environment. The mind decides what is harmful or what is desirable. When we feel we are under attack from something outside the body, we can react with fear or anger. We can also attack ourselves with thoughts of guilt and shame. When we attack, we activate the fight-or-flight sympathetic nervous system and secrete hormones and neurotransmitters that unleash electric currents, affecting the function of different body organs and systems.

We are not our body, however, and our body is also subject to our attack in the form of collateral damage. When we react in fear, grief, anger, or pride and defend ourselves against a perceived attack from others, our body suffers the consequences of our attack, and we suffer conditions such as hypertension, cardiac disease, cancer, arthritis, and chronic infection. When we attack ourselves with shame and guilt, we can develop autoimmune diseases. Therefore, in a way, our negative emotions attack our own body.

Process of Forgiveness

Forgiveness comes from the willingness to take the antidote to the poison that we drank or from letting go of the juice we received from self-righteousness. We get something out of holding onto our resentment. Otherwise, why would we want to keep it? Resentment is bolstered by pride, and pride is very powerful—but not always healthy.

The truth is, I can't make you do something you don't want to do, and you can't make me do something I don't want to do. If the phone rings, what do you do? Does the phone *make* you answer it, or are you *choosing* to answer it? So, if someone does something that makes you angry, who is making you angry? If you believe it is the other person that is actually making you angry, why do you give the other person so much power over you and allow them to make you angry and to upset your sense of well-being? It may be hard to accept the truth that anger, self-pity, self- righteousness, and resentment in dealing with a hurtful event is a *choice*. Forgiveness is a choice, as well.

Sometimes, we choose to take action because of a perceived injustice. Sometimes, we don't take action out of fear. There are other times we don't take action because we don't feel we deserve or are worthy of happiness. This causes stress from inner conflict. We can decide to leave a relationship based on anger or stay in a relationship based on fear. There is the dangerous desire to want revenge based on anger or pride. Decisions based on negative emotions are rarely the best decisions. Unless you are in a life-threatening situation, the best decision may be to *not* take action until greater understanding is gained.

In *The Four Agreements*, the second agreement Don Miguel Ruiz wrote was "Don't take things personally." It is the realization that when we feel bad, it is because we have taken on someone else's "stuff." It is not our stuff unless we choose to accept it. It may be that the person treats other people the same way or that we perceive we are under attack when that was not the intention.

We all have made mistakes. In *An Essay on Criticism,* Alexander Pope wrote, "To err is human; to forgive, divine." We all have done things in our lives out of ignorance that harm others more than we realize. Sometimes, we discount our transgression's significance, but that is what perpetrators frequently do. We have events occur in our lives that we consider tragic. There is never escape, however, from the consequences of the harm we've done to the lives of others.

A Course in Miracles is a spiritual text and workbook that teaches the reader that the way to healing, salvation, and miracles is through forgiveness. Forgiveness is the means to inner peace, freedom, and the highest levels of empowerment. Empowerment, however, is achieved through integrity (truth), personal responsibility, and compassion (forgiveness). Obstacles to forgiveness include being judgmental, self-righteousness, and prideful.

The antidote for resentment is forgiveness. Forgiveness comes from humility, compassion, courage, and surrender. It is the realization that by holding onto anger and resentment, I am actually hurting myself. It is the recognition that I am keeping that other person in my life and letting that person control me and make me sick. Humility is the unraveling of pride. It is the admission that I may not know the whole story. Compassion is the willingness to look at the event from another's perspective and try to understand that person's motive. What were they trying to get out of doing what they did? Oftentimes, their actions are based on their ignorance of what they thought was right or out of their own hurt. At times, I look at the other person throwing a temper tantrum like a three-year-old who didn't get his or her way.

Courage is the willingness to surrender one's own hurt to free oneself from the perpetrator. It is the willingness to let go of being right in exchange for being healthy. It takes greater courage to surrender one's pride and the juice one gets from holding onto anger and self- righteousness. Self-righteousness can make forgiveness difficult. Often, the desire for self- righteousness is so strong that it becomes even more powerful than life itself. Some people would rather die than give up their resentment and self-righteousness. Husbands murder their wives over being right. Countries go to war and destroy not only their enemies' lives but also the lives of their own countrymen out of self-righteousness. Only by surrendering the "payoff" of being right can one learn to forgive.

One of my pet peeves used to be being stuck in rush-hour traffic. I didn't mind an orderly merging of alternating vehicles onto a congested freeway from a freeway on-ramp. Cars that tried to speed ahead on the freeway shoulder to merge further down the freeway, however, or tried to squeeze in tightly behind another merging car used to made my blood boil. My girlfriend at the time told me of her boss's experience. His son had been troubled all his life, and one day, he found his son lying lifeless on the floor of his son's apartment. The ambulance was called and rushed the son to the emergency room. His father tried to follow the ambulance in his car but was stuck behind a slow-moving truck. Each time he tried to pass the truck, it would pull out in front of him to keep him from passing. Finally, he was able to accelerate past the truck, only to find the truck driver giving him "the finger" as he passed. The man drove to the emergency room in time to have the doctor pronounce his son dead.

After hearing that story, I developed much more patience for those impatient drivers who don't play by "my rules." Perhaps like that father, they are rushing off to some emergency or tragedy.

Self-Forgiveness

I have seen quite a few patients who are ill due to the inability for self-forgiveness. Oftentimes, it leads to addictions or other self-destructive behavior. The inability to forgive oneself is due to shame or guilt. Lack of self-forgiveness leads to anger being turned inward against oneself. Life energy is diverted from keeping one healthy to the intent of destroying oneself. There is a lack of self-worth and non-deservedness.

The inability to forgive ourselves is based on a powerful ego. Our actions and mistakes are greater than anyone else's. There are unrealistic high expectations for ourselves, leading to self-criticism and perfectionism. The inability for self-forgiveness frequently comes from overly critical parents or authority figures in childhood. The "truths" and beliefs we grew up with are based on falsehoods from the limited beliefs of others. We think what we are told is reality, but nothing could be further from the truth.

Sometimes, the inability to forgive ourselves is due to ignorance. We are ignorant to the fact that many others have made the same errors and mistakes. Everyone makes mistakes. No one can predict the future. When things don't work out as expected, we had no way of knowing. We don't have control over others or natural, inevitable events. Why should we hold ourselves to such higher standards than anyone else?

All conflicts involve the responsibility of both parties. It is never all just one person's fault. We blame the other person and don't take responsibility in the role we played in the conflict. Denial is not taking personal responsibility for one's own actions.

Sometimes, we bury our guilt in our subconscious, so it is not visible to the ego. We call that denial. The shame and self-condemnation are so great, they are not recognized—but they still affect us. A vast majority of our bodily functions are run by the subconscious, and the invisible guilt and shame can lead to illnesses without conscious awareness.

How much do we sacrifice ourselves for others in the name of compassion? Forgiveness doesn't necessarily mean being passive or accepting harmful action. A Tibetan Buddhist lama told a story of a woman who was being physically abused by her husband. After each abusive episode, the husband apologized and vowed it wouldn't happen again. It continued, however. Eventually, he even tried to convince his wife that she was also responsible for his actions. Out of both guilt and a sense of loyalty, the wife refused to leave her husband. She reasoned that she stayed in the relationship out of compassion, and she felt sorry for him. The lama was able to convince the woman that she was doing more harm to her husband's karma by staying in the marriage and allowing him to abuse her. In Christian terms, by leaving the marriage, she was helping her husband by preventing him from committing potentially greater sin that would keep him out of Heaven. Being compassionate, also means, being compassionate to yourself and removing yourself from a harmful situation.

At times, we hold ourselves personally responsible for other people's happiness, and if we think about our own needs, we feel guilty. We may have been taught by our parents that to be a "good boy" or "good girl" means we don't complain and keep quiet about our own needs. If we are hurt, our parents may just tell us to "suck it up" or "don't be a baby." We are taught to discount our own feelings. Sometimes, we are made to believe that we can only be loved if we are useful or that love has to be earned. Oftentimes, it leads to the belief that only by "doing" or buying loved ones gifts, can we prove our worth. Sometimes, this leads to overdoing for others to compensate for the lack of self-love and a feeling of inferiority. It has been said that you can't forgive another person until you forgive yourself. Some people have an easy time doing for others but have a hard time accepting help or kindness from others. That belief can come from feeling undeserving or unworthy, or from a sense of pride. Those beliefs and attitudes make self- healing impossible.

Forgiveness is about honoring one's own feelings of anger, shame, or guilt. It is beneficial, however, to realize that these emotions are not of the self but of the separate entity called ego. The ego is limited by its understanding. The ego is about punishment of self or others. Realize that your rules may not be other people's rules and that your rules are not enforceable to affect other people's behavior. Sometimes, our judgment involving hurts of the past can unfairly prejudice our beliefs in the present. We can generalize and mistakenly use absolute words like *all*, *always*, or *never*.

We are not our ego unless we think we are. The key is to not vilify the ego. Anger and hate just feed the ego and make it stronger. It is always easier to second-guess ourselves for past behavior once we see the consequences. It is pointless to feel guilty or ashamed about the mistakes we made when we were young and inexperienced. We always make the best choice we can given the circumstances and what we know at the time. The key is in gaining wisdom from the experience, and wisdom can't be gained without making mistakes. Self-forgiveness comes from accepting the reality that we are not perfect and do make mistakes.

Forgiving the Body

Our anger and resentment affect us more than the perceived perpetrator does. As mentioned, we are not the body, but the body's function is dictated by the mind. The war is going on inside the mind; the body is the innocent bystander, and disease is created. Forgiveness starts with the self. It is about disarming the inner judge and critic.

There are multimillion-dollar industries based on emotional insecurities about our bodies. We strive to improve our appearance through everything from hairstyles, cosmetics, and clothing to braces, liposuction, facelifts, Botox, anabolic steroid injections, bariatric surgery, and breast augmentation—all to improve our appearance. We think of our body as imperfect. We criticize our body as being too short, too tall, or too fat. Our face is too thin or too round; our nose is too big or too wide. We hate our body for the way it looks.

We hate our body even more when it's not healthy. If our body is injured or diseased, we become angry and try to dissociate from it or vilify it. Pain and disease are messengers, making us aware that something is wrong in our lives. We try to stifle the message so we can keep living the harmful habits that created the condition in the first place. Negative emotions that we hold in mind affect all the molecules, elements, cells, nerves, and energy flows of our bodies.

Potentially harmful sensations from the body or the environment send messages to the brain, causing stress. Stress triggers an emotional response of shame, guilt, grief, fear, anger, and resentment. We can suffer an injury or illness that can make us angry and resentful that it happened to us. We can become fearful or grieve that the injury will be physically disfiguring or disabling. We can feel guilty that we may have done something bad to deserve it. Physical pain increases emotional stress, and emotional stress increases perceived physical pain. Stress affects everyone differently. Stress speeds the aging process and makes the organs more susceptible to injury or disease. For some, it affects the heart; for others, it's the spine, gut, or lungs.

Instead of alienating the injured or diseased organ, listen to the message it is trying to communicate to your consciousness. The mind can lie through denial and resistance. Appreciate and respect the essence of what our body is trying to tell us. Our body is not the enemy but a reflection of thoughts. By changing our mind and changing our actions, we change our body. We heal by learning to forgive ourselves and our body for the way it is.

Finally, I want to emphasize that while beliefs and attitudes play an important role in self- healing, they are not the only factors. As mentioned in the chapter on awareness, the factors could be infinite. Eastern religions contribute these factors to *karma*. Your karma includes all you have inherited in genetics and physical susceptibilities. It also includes family beliefs and prejudices formulated in childhood and other more esoteric causes. One need not feel guilty or ashamed when one develops disease or is unable to heal. Everyone will eventually succumb to illness. A person can eat all the right foods and nutritional supplements, live in the most pristine environment, exercise, and work on growing spiritually and still develop disease. In the circle of life, with every beginning of life, there is an ending. I've heard it said that "life is a sexually transmitted disease in which the prognosis is terminal." Even the most enlightened beings who are free of emotional suffering have developed cancer and other diseases. Guilt is the shadow side of anger and resentment. Negative emotions work at the biochemical and physiologic level to impair the healing process. It is through forgiveness that we transcend guilt and find healing.

Exercises in Forgiveness

Exercise #1

1. **Focus on the breath and let go.** When we are angry or afraid, our physiology changes. We go into fight-or-flight mode, and our breathing becomes more shallow and rapid. Focus on breathing into the belly and think about someone you love.

2. **Accept the feeling without emotion or judgment.** Just focus on the feeling and remove the negative thoughts—or move them away from you.

3. **Become the witness/observer.** See yourself with the other person, as if witnessing the two of you in a movie or on stage in a play. Imagine what was running through the mind of the other person and what he or she was trying to get out of their actions. You may not like what the other person said or did, but identify their reasons. Remember how you felt at the time, and then grow yourself up to the age you are now. Think about how the older and wiser you would have thought about or handled the situation differently.

Exercise #2

Find the good when meeting others. In his book, *Teach Only Love: The Twelve Principles of Attitudinal Healing,* Dr. Gerald Jampolsky writes, "we seek only their innocence, not their guilt." By practicing looking for the good in others, we develop a more balanced perspective of the world. Look for the good qualities in the person you want to forgive.

Forgiveness can come out of compassion. It is seeing the other person as a human being. Forgiveness acknowledges that anger often comes from a cry for help, want of respect, or a call for love. With greater understanding, you may change the way you choose to interact with that person. But do not expect the other person to change. Remember, forgiveness is for you, not for the other person. What you seek is inner peace.

Exercise #3

"I release you, I forgive you, and I love you." This is a technique taught to me by Greywolf. Sometimes, the person we need to forgive is no longer in our lives, but our suffering persists. Write a letter to the perpetrator and include all your emotions and hurts. Make the letter as long as necessary until there is nothing left to write. When this is done, continue to write about how you forgive them. Then hold a ritual. Burn the letter, sending the letter from the physical to the non-physical realm. As it burns, say, "I release you, I forgive you, and I love you." You may be surprised by how well you sleep or how light you feel the next day.

CHAPTER EIGHT

Choice

"Life is a sum of all your choices."

—Albert Camus

"Allow the world to live as it chooses and allow yourself to live as you choose."

—Richard Bach

"The strongest principle of growth lies in human choice."

—George Elliot

"To decide to be at the level of choice is to take responsibility for your life and to be in control of your life."

—Abbie M. Dale

I first met William Glasser in 2002. After my divorce, I was having problems with my teenage son (imagine that!), and I had just broken up with my girlfriend. I just needed "a break" and wanted to get out of town for a while. I booked a room in a San Francisco hotel and drove down to the city late Friday night after I had finished work. The next day, I went for an early lunch at a restaurant in the hotel lobby. There was a long line of customers waiting to be seated, and I started a conversation with a woman who was in line in front of me. We got to the front of the line for seating, and she asked me if I might join her and her husband for lunch. I thanked her but told her that I didn't want to impose and would wait for the next table. But she insisted. I went with her to the table, and an older gentleman came to join us. She said, "I'd like you to meet my husband, William Glasser." I had no idea who William Glasser was, but I later learned from a psychologist and college professor friends that William Glasser was one of the world's greatest living psychiatrists. He had eleven institutes all over the world. His primary body of work focused on the treatment of children and adolescents. He was instrumental in developing counseling approaches in traditional and reform schools.

Dr. Glasser was to lecture at a conference at the hotel where I was staying, and he invited me to attend. He also gave me a copy of his latest book, *Warning; Psychiatry Can Be Dangerous to Your Mental Health.* There was one of the world's greatest living psychiatrists writing a book on the dangers of psychiatry. He believed that psychiatry should emphasize counseling and that psychiatry had lost its way. My experience in working in the hospital and requesting a psychiatry consult was that it was the primary emphasis of the psychiatrist to identify a DSM (*Diagnostic and Statistical Manual of Mental Disorders*) category and prescribe the most suitable medications. Counseling, for the most part, was delegated to psychologists, social workers, and counselors.

Even in psychiatry, treatment has become about the quick fix. In his book, Dr. Glasser talked about psychiatry selling out to the pharmaceutical companies. If a wife just lost her husband to cancer or a man lost his job and was depressed, a psychiatrist would prescribe a medication that would chemically alter the brain and cover up the depression, leaving the root cause of the depression untreated. The root cause would continue to alter neural-pathways so that, if the medication was discontinued, the depression would often return. Admittedly, there are inherent chemical imbalances that cause psychiatric conditions, which require medications. There are also times that the psychiatric condition is so severe that medications are required, in order to allow the patient to be able to do the cognitive work and also perform daily tasks. It has been shown in psychiatry, pain management, addiction medicine, and other fields of medicine, however, that medications by themselves don't work as well as concomitant counseling to resolve issues and beliefs, along with altering the patient's lifestyle. Without addressing the behavioral aspects, relapse often occurs.

Attending Dr. Glasser's lecture, I was impressed with the simplicity but effectiveness of his techniques. He invited me to study his counseling techniques with him and his wife, and for a year and a half, I ended up flying down to his home in Southern California for a weekend every other month. I have since used his techniques with many of my patients, which has resulted in a shift in their belief patterns to one of empowerment.

William Glasser said that what humans seek in life is happiness. Humans have five basic needs that, when fulfilled, lead to happiness. These are survival, love and belonging, fun, freedom, and power. Survival is having food, shelter, and other essentials for life. Fun comes from learning and doing something new. Freedom comes from having no limitations or controls. Power is control over oneself, others, or one's surroundings. What makes people the most happy is good relationships with others around them. Unhappiness comes from anger over not getting one's needs met in relationships. This leads to the use of external control. External control is trying to control the other person to make them do what you want them to do. External control involves using what Dr. Glasser calls the "seven deadly sins": blaming, nagging, threatening, criticizing, punishing, bribing, and complaining. Beyond childhood, no one can control another person. People want to have good, close relationships, but by using external control habits to meet our needs, we drive relationships apart. The way to improve relationships is to give up using external control on others in order to get needs met and instead making the relationship the top priority.

As opposed to traditional psychotherapy, which delves into childhood issues, Dr. Glasser believes in dealing with events and relationship issues in the *present*. His therapy focuses on changing a person's current thoughts and actions. Each person in the relationship puts aside individual desires for another entity called "the relationship," and each individual contributes to the support of the relationship. By only dealing with the present relationship, much counseling time is saved. Only if Dr. Glasser's therapy techniques are unsuccessful does he go to the client's childhood trauma or parental relationships.

The choices you make affect your relationship not only with others but also with yourself. More recently, Dr. Glasser has been integrating his work of reality therapy and choice theory into application in mind-body medicine, exploring the effects the mind has on physical health. He talked about his recent work with young adults suffering from juvenile-onset rheumatoid arthritis. He had group therapy with them for several weeks, and in the end, many of the participants were able to decrease their medications and were able to be more active. Dr. Glasser feels that arthritis is made worse by suppressed anger.

Dr. Glasser told me a story about a neighbor of his who asked him to treat her for her depression. Because she was a neighbor, he was reluctant, but because of her persistence, he finally agreed to treat her. She not only had depression but also severe rheumatoid arthritis. After a few sessions, he discovered that the root of her "depression" was actually suppressed anger toward her husband for something he had done to her in the past. Dr. Glasser counseled her for several weeks but was unable to get her to give up her anger. He finally told her that the only way she would stop feeling depressed was to leave her husband. Because of her fear and for financial reasons (they were very wealthy), she refused to leave her husband. After many failed attempts at resolution, Dr. Glasser told her there was nothing more he could do and ended his treatment with her. After some years, the women's husband died. Not only did her depression resolve but her arthritis remarkably improved.

The root cause of autoimmune diseases has perplexed scientists for years. Why does a body attack itself? Traditionally, genetic or molecular causes for autoimmune disease have been explored; only recently have holistic methods of psychological or spiritual approaches been studied.

Choice Theory

As previously mentioned, health is dependent on three factors: genetics, environment, and behavior. In explaining choice theory, Dr. Glasser utilizes the metaphor of a car to help with understanding the relationship of the mind and body. He defines the driver of your car (body) as "total behavior," which is powered by "basic needs" (car engine). The four wheels metaphorically represent different aspects of the mind and body. The body's "physiology" and the mind's "feelings" are the back wheels of the car. "Thinking" and "acting" are the front wheels. The back wheels are fixed and can only go in one direction (Figure 2). In other words, you can't control your physiology (disease or pain), and you can't control your feelings. The steering wheel, however, is able to turn the front wheels to the left or right. You are the driver of the car and can choose which direction the car goes by turning the steering wheel to turn the front wheels. You can choose the way you think, and you can choose the way you act. Imagine yourself choosing not to take the steering wheel and continuing in the same direction on the same path for the next five to ten years. Where would you be? How does it look? How does it feel? What would be different about your life? You can choose to continue on the same path, or you take the steering wheel and create a new path for yourself. You have the choice of living your life the way you have been living it up to now or changing your life to the one you want to have.

WHERE YOU ARE GOING

WHERE YOU WANT TO GO

THINKING

BASIC NEEDS

ACTING

TOTAL BEHAVIOR

FEELING

PHYSIOLOGY

Figure 2: Glasser's Car

As the driver of your life, only you have the power to change your life. You have the choice to continue looking in the rear-view mirror of all the hurts in your life, or you can look out the front windshield to the road ahead and where you want your future to take you.

As humans, we are very creative beings and can choose to create the reality we want. We can choose how we see the world. Many times we identify ourselves with the choices we make. If we feel depressed, we think we are the depression or "being depressed." If we feel angry, we identify ourselves as "being angry." We become our emotions.

We are more than how we feel, however. We have to remember that we are not the choices we make. We can choose to be angry or depressed or any other emotion. Our emotions are based on how we see the world and how we react to things that happen to us, but *we are not the emotion or feeling*. It makes it more difficult to change how we feel if we think we are the emotions we feel, as opposed to realizing that we are choosing to act depressed or angry. Instead of saying, "I am depressed or angry," we can say, "I am depressing or angering as a form of action, like I am running or eating." We know we have a choice to keep running or eating. Likewise, we have a choice to keep depressing or angering.

People are always wanting what is good (i.e., to lose weight, stop drinking, or spend more time with family). After New Year's Day, the athletic club is crowded with people having positive intentions, but attendance progressively declines over time. There are New Age practices promoting the power of attraction to get what you want in life through intention. The power of intention aligns thought and mind toward a specific goal. The new intended goal and direction, however, wouldn't have been initiated unless a person took responsibility to choose and do something different.

There are many who want something different but keep living their lives without any change. According to a well-known saying, the definition of insanity is doing the same thing over and over again and expecting a different result. The choices we make each instant direct behavior toward the desired outcome. We can choose to set a new destination and take action toward it. We don't realize our true potential until we empower ourselves with the power of choice. Choice moves us from potential to reality.

Many people believe they deserve more than they have. The truth is they deserve *exactly* what they have. They are living their potential based on the choices they made until now. The way we are in the present is the unfolding of our potential at that moment. Choice can only occur in the present. The power to manifest occurs only in the *now*. By making different choices, we redefine who we are.

Exercise in Dr. Glasser's Reality Therapy

The truth is that no one can make you do anything you don't want to do, and you can't make someone else do something they don't want to do. You are responsible for making the changes you want to see in your life. Ask yourself the following questions:

1. What do I want?

2. What am I doing?

3. Is what I am doing getting me what I want?

4. What can I do differently to get what I want?

When setting a different course in life, the question "What do I want?" can be difficult. It was a difficult question for me when I finally realized I wasn't happy and needed to make changes in my life. I was so beaten down and entrenched in what I was doing that I never allowed myself to think differently and dream. The question "What makes me excited?" might be better. In other words, what brings a warm feeling to your heart and raises your energy level just by thinking about it? It is the energy of the feeling that is able to motivate you and pushes you forward—even when times get tough.

Dr. Glasser's reality therapy is also good for using with acquaintances and family who play the role of the victim. Instead of buying in with listening to someone's sob story for the thousandth time, you make them responsible for making changes in their own lives. First, inspire and empower them. Say, "Sue, you are a resourceful person and have a lot going for you. What do you want, and what can you do differently to get what you want?" This makes the other person responsible for making changes in her own life.

CHAPTER NINE

Responsibility and Empowerment

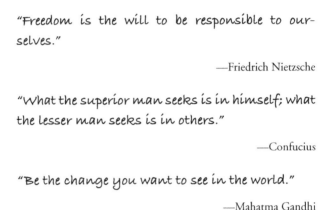

"Freedom is the will to be responsible to ourselves."

—Friedrich Nietzsche

"What the superior man seeks is in himself; what the lesser man seeks is in others."

—Confucius

"Be the change you want to see in the world."

—Mahatma Gandhi

I met Tom Ballestieri in Santa Fe at a conference in which he was speaking. He was giving a talk called "The Responsibility of Elders." He had spent several years with the Lakota Sioux in the Dakotas, learning their culture and wisdom. He is Italian-American by descent but had become so involved with the Lakota Sioux culture that he was eventually awarded one of their highest honors as an Uweepee medicine man. He recounted an incident in which he was to be the fire tender of a sweat lodge ceremony: a sacred event of purification in the Native American culture. The fire tender's job is important in maintaining and monitoring the fire that is heating the rocks to be used in the ceremony. The day Tom was to be the fire tender was an exceptionally hot one, and standing by the raging fire made the heat that much more sweltering. He was sweating profusely and began feeling faint. He needed to get relief from the sun and heat, but there was no shade except for a small tree around the other side of the sweat lodge. He just needed a few minutes in the shade, he thought, and collapsed under the shadow of the tree. Suddenly, after resting a few minutes, he began to see smoke and smell the burning of material from the direction of the fire. He quickly got to his feet and ran over to the fire, where he realized the sweat lodge had caught on fire. As he worked to try and put the fire out, many of the Lakota Sioux elders (including his teacher, Joe Eagle Elk) saw the smoke and ran down the ridge to where Tom stood with the burning structure.

"Oh, Tom," Joe Eagle Elk said, "you caught the sweat lodge on fire."

To his chagrin, Tom hung his head and related the details of what had happened and remorsefully admitted to Joe Eagle Elk, "It was all my fault."

"No, Tom," Joe Eagle Elk replied, "it's not your fault. It was my fault. I could have taught you the way a fire should be built. I could have taught you that if the wind blows, a wind break should be built. It was my fault for not teaching you properly."

The message of the story is that we have much to learn from the wisdom of the indigenous people that live close to the Earth. Joe Eagle Elk did not blame Tom for the accident; he took responsibility for not being a good enough teacher. In our society, there is a growing lack of personal responsibility for one's actions. It's much easier to blame someone else or something else for the poor situation in which one finds oneself. Oftentimes in this world, there is a competition to become the greater victim. We find parents who are unwilling to take responsibility for the behavior of their children. They blame the schools or teachers they expected would teach their children, but they don't hold the children themselves accountable. Laws get written to empower the child: to excuse disrespectful behavior with no responsibility or consequences. I've talked to a number of teachers who have taught anywhere from twenty to thirty years, and they all say the same thing: Over the past several years, the children have become more disrespectful of authority and have a greater sense of entitlement.

There is the belief that it is someone else's responsibility to improve not only our lives but also the plight of the world. We become victims, and we don't take personal responsibility for making the changes that would make our lives better. Often, people who blame take the least responsibility for their actions or situations; they are also often the ones who live in the greatest poverty and disempowerment. It is up to each person to be responsible for oneself and one's actions. In our society, we tend to blame others for where we are in life. It is the responsibility of each of us to be a role model—instead of looking to someone or something else to make a difference.

In the Iroquois tradition, tribal decisions are made that not only affect the present generation but also the six generations to follow. In our current culture, there is a tendency to want immediate gratification. There are too few decisions that look at the long-term effects of personal or political choices—choices that may provide short-term benefit but be disastrous in the long run. By taking into consideration how our actions will affect us over time and how those actions might impact others, we make better decisions.

Victim/Villain/Hero

Mark Saito, a *kahuna* with whom I studied, told a story about how he learned of the "triad." Mark's father was Japanese and a renowned martial artist. Mark's mother was Hawaiian and taught Mark the way of the *huna*, the art of Hawaiian mysticism. Mark recalled an edifying story when he was a young man. He was making a purchase at a convenient store in Honolulu when he looked out the front store window and saw a man and woman shouting angrily at each other. Suddenly, the man took his hand and slapped the woman across the face, knocking her to the sidewalk. Mark went out to defend the woman and told the man he shouldn't be hitting her. The man then turned his attention and anger to Mark and attacked him. The *kahuna* defended himself but did damage to the boyfriend in the process. Suddenly, Mark began to experience pain in his body and heard screaming coming from behind him. He turned and found that the man's girlfriend had jumped on Mark's back and had begun scratching him, biting him, ripping at his clothes, and gouging him. Bewildered, Mark backed away from the situation and escaped to the dojo where his father was giving a martial arts class. Upon seeing his son bleeding with his clothes torn and hair disheveled, his father asked Mark what had happened. Upon hearing the story, Mark's father began to laugh and explained about the triad of the hero, victim, and villain.

As Jaques explains in William Shakespeare's *As You Like It*:

> [T]he world is a stage,
> And all the men and women merely players;
> They have their exits and their entrances,
> And one man in his time plays many parts …

A person's judgment and self-righteousness can create a drama that is very addicting. Steven Karpman originated the Karpman drama triangle. In human relationships, a person assumes one of three characters: the hero (rescuer), the villain (perpetrator), or the victim. A person alternates between the three roles at different times and in different situations. While a person may choose to play one role, ironically, other participants can simultaneously view the person in a different role. A hero to one would be a perpetrator or villain to another.

At the convenience store, Mark entered the drama thinking he was the hero. He was rescuing the girl (whom he perceived to be the victim) from the boyfriend (whom he perceived to be the villain). After entering the drama, however, the girl perceived Mark to be the villain, as he was beating up her boyfriend, whom she perceived to be the victim. The girl saw herself as the hero protecting her boyfriend.

Everything depends on personal subjective perspective. This menagerie of roles can happen in other relationships at work, between friends, or between nations. That's why wars are fought: Each side judges themselves to be right. People become addicted to being right and think their opinion is the only right one. Self-righteousness has led to more loss of human life throughout history than any other cause, including plagues and natural disasters.

There is an attraction to interacting with others and playing a role in the drama. Like Mark, heroes can act with good intention, but their acts may be seen as villainous by others. Heroes want to feel good about themselves, and they think of themselves as much greater than they are. The hero (rescuer) wants to experience gratitude and adulation from others. The heroes live in pride and self-righteousness, thinking they know what's best for everyone. Heroes take responsibility for others but not for themselves.

The villain, or perpetrator, often comes from a critical parent who acted out of anger and was unyielding. The villain oppresses the victim with blame and criticism. Sometimes, we blame ourselves as villains when we act with good intentions that nevertheless end in a bad outcome. Viewing ourselves as the villain may lead to accepting criticism and blame from others. We think of ourselves as much worse than we actually are and develop self-hatred, shame, and guilt. In doing so, we turn ourselves from a perceived villain into a victim in our mind, which can lead to blame, anger and fear. Self-appointed villains are actually egotistical and view their actions as so egregious as to transcend into other aspects of their lives. They feel that their actions are so important as to even turn God against them.

We all have played the victim at some time in our lives. Victims believe there are outside forces preventing them from getting what they want—or giving them things they don't want. They may say, "What's the use?", and live lives in learned helplessness. By being a victim, one doesn't have to assume any personal responsibility.

How do you know when you are playing a victim? You are a victim if you blame others for your situation and have self-pity. You are a victim if you think of yourself as helpless or your situation as hopeless. You are a victim if you are looking for someone else to fix your problem. Defensiveness arises from being a victim. If you think you are vulnerable to attack, you can become defensive and attack in return.

In society, it can pay to be a victim. Victims look for sympathy and pity from others to give them things. They reap secondary gains from their victimhood and a belief about their self-identity. It is learned behavior or a belief about one's self-identity. Victims tend to identify themselves by their illness or their trauma. A victim by definition is a powerless person. A person with an illness who is also a victim will have no power to heal.

People who deal with victims often find it exhausting. Victims always look for heroes or someone to rescue them. Victims may use praise to trigger the hero's pride and get what the victim wants. Victims may try to blame the rescuer in order to trigger guilt and shame to get what the victim wants. The hero gives his or her energy to pick the victim up, but the victim falls down again. The hero picks the victim up, and the victim falls down again. *Taking energy* is the basis of the relationship. The person, who is always taking energy from others and getting what he or she wants, never wants to leave the relationship and never wants the relationship to change. We call that narcissism. Victims will always want to remain victims in order to take power, and it is the caregiver (rescuer) who develops disease. Victims are energy vampires who don't want to use their own energy to get out of their predicament; rather, they look for someone else to do it for them. After a while, the rescuer's energy is drained, and he or she is resentful of the victim's behavior. When the rescuer finally decides not to help the victim anymore, the victim directs a role change, and the rescuer becomes the villain.

Being a victim impairs healing. Insurance statistics have shown that people who have injuries and a pending lawsuit don't respond as well to treatment and can take twice as long to heal. This can occur even without conscious awareness or malingering. The barrier to healing is held in the subconscious.

The Martyr

New Oxford American Dictionary defines *martyr* as:

- a person who displays or exaggerates their discomfort or distress in order to obtain sympathy or admiration ("She wanted to play the martyr.");
- (martyr to) a constant sufferer from (an ailment) ("I'm a martyr to migraines!").

Heroes (rescuers) can also be identified as martyrs or do-gooders. People who act as martyrs have an internal drama or conflict. They view themselves simultaneously as hero and victim. Martyrdom is going against oneself by taking from the self and giving to others out of a sense of obligation. A child, spouse, or parent uses blame, guilt, and shame against the martyr to get what he or she wants. Parents are common martyrs. We love our children and see them as special. Oftentimes, we see our children as a reflection of ourselves, and we become afraid the world will judge us if they fail. We sacrifice ourselves to get them to be what we hope they will be. The common question is, "They're my children, and I want to help them, but when is enough, enough?"

It is a conflict between loyalty and integrity. A person has to ask himself or herself, "Am I doing this out of love or obligation?" By constantly doing for someone else even though he is a loved one, are you really helping him or making him more dependent and handicapped? The second question is, "Am I doing it for the other person, or am I doing it for myself?" Are you doing it because you're expecting something in return, such as appreciation? Is it self-serving, and do you think about how wonderful you are for doing it as you await the applause? Doing something out of love means never expecting anything in return. It is not about "what a wonderful wife I am" or "what a wonderful mother I am." It takes self-honesty and courage to arrive at the truth.

It takes a lot of courage to change roles in the drama from hero (or rescuer) to perpetrator (or villain), even though these roles are an illusion. It is about changing your self-worth based on honoring and respecting yourself for who you are—not for what you do or for what others think of you. It is all based on perspective and therefore should not be judged by any observer. It is about breaking old belief patterns and living in health and integrity. In terms of our role as parents, we are responsible for making sure our children are well-equipped with the values and beliefs that allow them to survive and be happy in life. Our role is not about preventing them from experiencing failures or pain; it is about taking responsibility for life's lessons that lead to personal growth.

Fibromyalgia is a disease that is common to martyrs. It is a condition in which the entire body—skin, muscles, and joints—are in pain. People who suffer with fibromyalgia tend to have certain characteristics. The majority of the patients are women. Frequently, there is a history of childhood trauma, which can occur from a lack of childhood love and nurturing from the mother. It can also occur from childhood sexual, physical, or emotional abuse. The abuse is ignored or hidden by the family out of a sense of shame or loyalty to the perpetrator, who may be a parent or other family member. The trauma oftentimes never gets addressed. It is resisted or denied but not resolved, and it festers in the mind. Do you stay loyal by continuing the secrecy to protect others, or do you honor yourself? Do you act as if nothing happened, even though deep down you know it did, and it is affecting your health?

Another characteristic of the fibromyalgia patient is that they tend to not give 100%, but rather 150% all the time. There is a tendency to be overactive in "doing." Suppressed trauma leads to anxiety, which turns into nervous energy and insomnia. The mind is hyperactive with thoughts, and the body is hyperactive with activities to bury past wounds and prevent those memories from coming into consciousness. There is a loss of integrity: Outwardly, the patient chooses to appear happy in order to disguise the buried emotional pain. Due to shame and lack of self-worth, patients can become addicted to drugs, alcohol, exercise, food, or even to "doing"—all in order to block the emotional pain. Victims will try to compensate by being the hero and "overdo" as the martyr. Since they are resisting against themselves, however, it is a conflict (or war) that cannot be won. The more they resist with suppression and repression, the stronger the anxiety or stress becomes. Thought precedes form. The inner war spreads from the mind into the body and is experienced as pain and disease. The physical pain distracts from the emotional pain. Treating the physical symptoms will not treat the root of the disease, which is in the mind. A person can even be involved in a drama triad with parts of themselves. Why does the mind look at disease as an attacker and separate from the self? I relate this to the rescuer/villain/victim triad that traps people in life drama. People tend to view themselves as their body or their mind. A person hates their body because it is not what they think it should be: "I'm too fat," "I'm ugly," "My breasts are too small," etc. A woman who was a victim of childhood sexual abuse may vilify her gender, sexual genitalia, or sexuality. During a time of illness, a person may hate the injury or disease, which is a part of his or her body. The body or the disease is the villain, and the mind is the victim. How does one defeat a part of oneself? How does one overcome the perceived enemy and inner conflict?

To transcend the drama triangle, one must first understand that the triangle is just a game. The game is about getting control over another or over oneself. The hero tries to control the victim and villain to get the outcome the hero wants. The victim tries to control the rescuer (hero) with pity and praise, and the villain with guilt and blame. I have had patients who become sick with exhaustion trying to rescue entitled children or demanding elderly parents. Sometimes, family members will team up to vilify a member of the family in an attempt to control the villain. A villain can also be designated as someone who decides to not participate in the drama.

People may also play the triangle in their own mind. They may think of themselves as villains and beat themselves up with guilt and shame. They may think of themselves as victims and live in anger and fear. Martyrs play both characters at the same time and live in obligation, which drains life's energy. Ultimately, playing the drama can affect a person's health.

There is a difference between acting as a rescuer versus acting out of compassion. The rescuer tries to control the behavior of others and tries to control the outcome. Compassion does neither. When someone acts out of compassion, there is no need for praise. It is all about acting out of kindness without gain.

In order to facilitate healing, one has to want to get out of the role as victim or villain. Diseases are attached to certain roles we play. The book *A Course in Miracles* says, "Healing is accomplished the instant the sufferer no longer sees any value in pain (or disease)." Victims don't like to see themselves as responsible. It would mean that blame can no longer be used, and that is a hard thing for victims to accept. They would be admitting that they are choosing the way they are and are ultimately responsible for their illness.

No one can heal you but yourself. In order to heal, you have to be responsible for your thoughts. It takes great courage to overcome guilt and accept the truth that part of you wants to have the disease because of secondary gains. With inner honesty, you can identify the secondary gains that keep the illness in place. With acceptance of responsibility and willingness to give up the secondary gains, the illness becomes healed.

Power and Personal Responsibility

As we discussed in the previous chapter on choice, it is your responsibility to make different choices to improve your health and life. Dr. Glasser, in using his choice theory, would often say, "I can't make you do something you don't want to do. If someone does something that makes you angry—and no one can make you do something you don't want to do—who is making you angry?"

As we previously discussed, your emotions affect your health. The key to healing is to be responsible for your feelings and your healing. Assuming personal responsibility is both the most challenging and the most rewarding thing a person can do in achieving their own empowerment. I remember the line from the Spiderman movie, "with great power comes great responsibility," but it is also true that with great responsibility comes great power. Thought, word, and action all have the potential to have great power to do good when used in truth, but they can also be very destructive when used in falsehood. By taking responsibility to change the mind and heal one's reality, the body heals.

We can't rely on others to change our conditions for us. No one can change us but ourselves. No one can heal us but ourselves, and it starts with setting the intention, taking personal responsibility, and persevering. Positive attitude and motivation can have a tremendous effect on improving your body's ability to heal from infection, cancer, and surgery by enhancing the immune system. A positive attitude helps one to overcome disease, allows peace of mind, and slows aging. Changes occur not from *knowing about* but from *becoming* the change. Being responsible helps one transcend the level of consciousness that created the disease. Awareness is about the mental and spiritual aspect of allowing change. Responsibility is about turning awareness into action in manifesting change in the body.

Exercise:

1. With conflicts in your relationships, think about which role you play. Do you play the role of the hero, the villain, or the victim? Do you want to stay in that role in the drama, or do you actually want to stay in the drama? In dealing with people who want to be victims, I offer compassion but ask them, "What can you do for yourself to improve your situation?"

2. Do you have the courage to ask yourself the hard question? What are you getting out of being sick or from being in the situation you don't want? We have to take some responsibility for where we are. We all have a secondary gain for being in the situation we are in. We can deny this, but it is truth.

CHAPTER TEN

Belief and Consciousness

"Believe nothing just because a so-called wise person said it.
Believe nothing just because a belief is generally held.
Believe nothing just because it is said in ancient books.
Believe nothing just because it is said to be of divine origin. Believe nothing just because someone else believes it.
Believe only what you yourself test and judge to be true."

—Buddha

"We have not lost faith, but we have transferred it from God to the medical profession."

—George Bernard Shaw

"The body is a reflection of what we believe. Our fear is based in our beliefs."

—Bernie Siegel

We base our actions on our beliefs. Our beliefs are based on our perceptions. How much of what we perceive is reality? How many times while driving on a desert highway do we think we see the mirage of water on the road ahead? The chair on which you might be sitting seems quite solid. Science, however, would tell you that it is 99.999% empty space. I was taught in school that the smallest components of all things are made of atoms, and the basic structure of the atom consists of a nucleus with a positive electrical charge, along with small, negatively charged electrons that orbit around the nucleus like planets around the sun. If the nucleus were to be expanded to the size of a soccer ball, the nearest electron would encircle a football stadium.

With all this empty space, why can't I put my hand through a perceived solid object? Are you sitting still while reading this book, or are you traveling over a 1,000 miles per hour as Earth spins on its axis and rotates around the sun, which moves in the galaxy as the universe expands?

Just because we don't perceive or experience something doesn't mean it doesn't exist. There are sounds such as a dog whistle that cannot be detected by the human ear. There are others who experience perceptions most people don't. There are individuals who have such an exquisite palate that they are able to distinguish ingredients in food or drink. Michelangelo saw the figure of David in a slab of granite and claimed all he did was get the statue "out." I am unable to see TV waves or hear radio waves even though they convert to perceptible energy when they enter my television, radio, or cell phone.

Perceptions can be deceptive. An article in the journal Neurology on 1/28/15 published by Albert J. Espay et. al. at the University of Cinncinati performed a study in which two placebos were given to 12 patients with moderate to severe Parkinson's disease. There was no difference between the two placebos except the patients were told that one was 15 times more expensive than the other "drug." The subjects reported the more expensive drug worked better.

I recall a story of Colin Turnbull, a cultural anthropologist, who took a Pygmy chief out of the tropical rainforest. In the rainforest, there is nothing but the sky above in which the birds fly and the ground below one's feet. The foliage is so thick that one can't see beyond a few feet in any direction. Colin Turnbull took the Pygmy chief to a knoll overlooking a great plain. The chief laughed when he saw animals in the distance that were no bigger than beetles, but he then became distraught when the animals started walking toward them and appeared to grow larger and larger in size. Colin Turnbull then took the Mbuti Pygmy chief to the hotel where they would be staying. He had the chief wait in the lobby while Turnbull took the elevator up to their room for a moment. Soon after the elevator door closed, the doors reopened, and two women stepped out into the lobby. Later that night when it was time to go upstairs to their room, the Pygmy chief refused to get into the elevator because he didn't want to be turned into two women.

Almost all of our beliefs get formed early in childhood. Rema Laibow wrote a research paper in quantitative EEG and neurofeedback. An electroencephalogram (EEG) measures the electrical activity of the brain. Brain waves are measured in hertz (cycles per second). The faster the cycles or frequency, the greater the brain activity. He studied the EEG patterns of children from birth into early adolescents. He found that from infancy to two years of age, the brain waves are at their slowest, running at 0.5 to 4 hertz (Hz). These are called delta waves. From two to six years of age, the brain waves increase to 4 to 8 Hz. These are called theta waves. From ages older than six and into adolescence, the brain waves continue to increase in frequency. Alpha waves from 8–12 Hz occur when an adult is at a calm and conscious state. Beta waves from 12–35 Hz start to occur at age twelve during reading and sedentary mental activities. Gamma waves greater than 35 Hz occur during peak performance activities. It has been found that in deep meditative or hypnotic states, a person is most suggestible and easily influenced. The measured brain waves in this condition run between 4 and 8 Hz—the same brain pattern that occurs in ages two to six. This is why new learning, such as a foreign language or skiing, is so much easier at a young age, rather than as an adult. The child's brain is most open to learning new information but is unable to distinguish right data from wrong in forming beliefs. So much of how we think of ourselves and the world as adults is carried over from the beliefs of our parents and the experiences we have at our youngest, most impressionable stage of life. All corporate marketers know this fact. In our society, more than half of all children are raised in single-parent households, and the mother is the primary caregiver. Television has become the number-one babysitter for our youth. After a full day at work, the mother will place the child in front of the television while she makes dinner and performs household tasks. Marketers use television shows and commercials to program the child's mind toward their product and consumerism. It has been shown that there is a direct link between childhood obesity, attention deficit hyperactivity disorder (ADHD) and watching television at age three and younger (DA Christakis, 2004).

Beliefs affect changes in our body. Those beliefs may have no basis in reality. Imagine biting into a sour lemon. Your mouth begins to water, and your lips may start to pucker. One can have a nightmare or a scary thought. The heart rate speeds up, the skin can become sweaty or clammy, and the muscles get tense. Can our beliefs, however, cause illness or assist in healing?

In 1957, Bruno Klofler in the *Journal of Projective Techniques* cited the case of "Mr. Wright," who was a man dying of cancer of the lymph nodes. He had tumors all over his body, including his neck, chest, and abdomen. He was essentially bedridden and was struggling just to breathe. His doctors had exhausted all the conventional treatments without success. Finally, they offered him one last option: an experimental drug called Krebiozen. The doctors convinced him that the drug had shown great promise. He agreed to take the medication, and within three days of receiving his first injection, he was cheerful, joking with nurses, and walking down the hospital floors. After ten days, his tumors had shrunk to half their original size, and he was discharged home. Two months later, however, there were news reports questioning the efficacy of Krebiozen. Mr. Wright suffered a relapse. His doctors told him there was a new, more effective version of Krebiozen, although in truth, it was the same drug. Upon completing the second course of the drug, he improved even more than he had following the first course of the drug and walked out of the hospital symptom-free. He remained symptom-free for two months, after which he read reports that Krebiozen was worthless. He ended up dying within days.

Bruce Moseley is an orthopedic surgeon in Texas and an associate professor at Baylor University School of Medicine. Dr. Moseley thought he was providing a great service to his patients by performing arthroscopic surgery on their arthritic knees. He decided to do a research experiment to objectify the benefits he saw in his patients. One group received the usual arthroscopic procedure with debridement of the arthritis. A second group received arthroscopy, but the knee joint was just irrigated with normal saline. The third group had a sham surgery: Patients were taken into the operating room, put under anesthesia with routine prep and sounds, then given a skin incision. No actual surgery was performed, however. The results were unexpected and found that the outcomes were almost identical for all three groups. The patients who received the sham surgery did just as well as those who received the routine arthroscopic surgery.

How much do our beliefs limit us? It was once believed as fact that a man could not run a mile faster than four minutes. Many had tried, and all had failed. It wasn't until Roger Bannister shattered the barrier that suddenly, many others realized it was possible and were able to surpass the barrier, as well. World records in both track-and-field and swimming continue to be broken. It is now uncertain what is achievable by the human once we eliminate the limitations of our old belief patterns.

Our beliefs create our view of the world and contribute to our level of consciousness. Some of our beliefs may serve us well. Other beliefs, appropriate in the past and under different circumstances, no longer serve us in the present—and may actually be detrimental. Our old beliefs can cause fears and desires of events that haven't happened and may not happen. Anger, guilt, and grief from events in the past can lead to unhappiness and emotional pain in the present. We can change our perspective and old beliefs with intention and courage. With awareness, we can find the truth about a belief.

Exploration of consciousness is the next scientific frontier. How much of our consciousness is spent in the present moment? How many of our thoughts are negative and focused on the past or future? In the previous chapters, we discussed that only thoughts based in truth have any power. Lies are illusory and have no foundation in reality. Because lies aren't real, they have no power to heal. The same can be said for the concepts of time. The past existed at one time but no longer exists in the present. As hard as we wish, we can't make ourselves twenty-one again, bring back deceased loved ones, or undo traumatic events that happened in our lives. We are different people than we were in the past. 98% of the atoms that make up our bodies get replaced every year. We grow, mature, and gain wisdom.

With our change in thoughts and beliefs, it may be possible to remodel the body in a different way. A true measure of whether I am headed in the right direction is if I feel I'm much better off at present than I was in the past. We frequently base our course of action on the experiences we had in the past. If certain behaviors were rewarding, they tend to be repeated, and behaviors that led to pain or tragedy tend to be avoided. Oftentimes, our memories get distorted with time. I have seen people from my past who looked so big when I was a child, and then later in life, they looked quite different. When we are children, everything and everyone in the world looks so big. Our memories of relationships can be greatly exaggerated for the better or worse based on our attitude. A sentimental and loving relationship memory can trivialize the past events of fighting and hurt feelings. A child's painful memory of parental punishment or restriction can override the positive parental intent to protect the child. In every good there is bad, and in every bad there is good. Physiology is affected by both positive and negative feelings. Positive feelings add to your health and sense of well-being. Negative feelings have the affect on a quantum and cellular level to cause disease.

Our perceptions of the future are also affected by the past. Worry and fear are feelings about the future. We don't worry about or fear things that have happened already. Worry and fear of things in the future leads to anxiety. Depression arises from a sense of hopelessness of a positive future. Going through life in vigilance makes one look for things that will cause harm in the future—instead of appreciating the beauty of life in the present. The future hasn't been written yet and is illusory. There is a Yiddish proverb that states, "Man plans and God laughs." How often have things worked out in our life's journey exactly like we planned? What we want out of life changes with time. When I was six years old, I wanted to be Superman. When I was twelve, I wanted to be a secret agent (à la James Bond), and when I was fourteen, I dreamed of being a professional football quarterback. These were childhood fantasies of how things I wanted would make me happy. Do we end up doing or having things in life we thought would make us happy? It takes looking at the past differently to rewrite how we see the future.

False beliefs can come from misinterpretation of perceptions, living in the past or future, and our attitude. How do we get to that desired outcome? It comes from introspection and inner honesty. Imagine oneself having accomplished that outcome or desired state. What does it look like or sound like? How does it feel? How will it affect your life or those around you? What are you willing to give up to get that desired state?

One of my teachers, Robert Dilts, says there is a present state (how things are) and a desired state (how we want our life in the future). We need resources to get us from where we are to where we want to be. Resources can be a person, place, or thing. The person can be a teacher or mentor. The place can be a school, a new job, or a more supportive environment. The thing can be more information, time, or money. The goal would be to make a list of the needed rsources one needs to achieve our desired goal.

Start by writing down the details of your desired goal and how it will change your life. Write about your vision of what it will look like, sound like, or feel like when you accomplish it. It is the strength of the feeling of having the desired state that is the motivating power. If you can't picture it or see yourself living it, you won't be able to achieve it.

Sometimes, the task can seem overwhelming so that we don't know where to start or even question if it can be done. It makes us want to give up. This, however, is just a limiting belief. When things seem so overwhelming, we can break the task into smaller and smaller components, or "chunk down." We can decide the first small steps to take that will get us going. What can I accomplish today? What can I accomplish by next week? What do I want to have done by next year? It is best to journal. It is like writing out a business plan and making things more real and tangible.

Write down short-term and long-range goals—and a realistic time frame to get them accomplished. Write about the resources (both short- and long-term) needed each step of the way. Think about the resources you will need right away and the others you can get later. By setting the intention, our consciousness automatically starts to locate and attract resources we need to obtain our desired outcome.

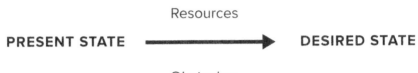

We have discussed resources that are needed to achieve a desired outcome. There is also interference (or obstacles) to getting what we want. These are: 1.) we don't know how; 2.) we think other people can do it, but we don't think we can; and 3.) part of us doesn't really want to achieve our goal. We may not whole-heartedly want to achieve the goal. It may be because we are unwilling to sacrifice the amount of time and effort needed, or maybe it really wasn't that important to us in the first place. Maybe there is a fear of failure. Perhaps there is the belief that we don't deserve or are unworthy of achieving our desire. There may also be secondary gains we receive from keeping things as they are. We may be comfortable with the way things are right now and really don't want change. We may not be willing to have a change in our relationships that may occur if we go after our dreams.

The book *A Course of Miracles* discusses self-healing from disease. The first step in self-healing begins with the realization that we have the capacity to heal ourselves, and there is no greater level of difficulty in the healing, regardless of the disease. There is no more difficulty in healing an autoimmune disease than there is in healing acne. The levels of difficulty in healing are just your limited (or false) beliefs. Self-healing involves the willingness and courage to give up old beliefs that created the disease in the first place. It takes inner honesty in asking questions like:

- What are my beliefs doing for me?
- What am I getting out of being sick?
- Is my illness keeping me from facing my fears?
- Is my unwillingness to heal due to unconscious guilt and wanting to punish myself by being sick?
- Am I doing it for other people in my life?
- Am I sick out of anger at others and trying to make them feel guilty?
- Am I getting benefit in attention and sympathy from others with my illness?

If you cannot come up with an answer to these questions, then you are not being honest with yourself. It takes a great deal of inner honesty to admit that one is contributing to one's illness. You need courage to surrender who you thought you were and to change your beliefs in order to change your body and health.

Exercise

1. Set your intention. Where do you want to be in five years? Think positive, not about what you *don't* want (i.e., to not have pain or not be sick). Ask yourself what you want instead. Ask yourself why you want it. Ask yourself what it would do for you once you are able to achieve your goal. Ask yourself, "And then what?" Ask these questions over and over again to build momentum.

2. Allow yourself to experience what that desired state looks like, sounds like, and feels like. Feel where it starts in your body and magnify the feeling with each breath, so it circulates and encompasses your entire body. This is the energy to keep you motivated and focused. The stronger the motivation, the greater chance of achieving it. Go back to that feeling as often as you need to in order to stay motivated.

3. Is there anything that holds you back? Address those issues and see if they are real or can they be resolved. What are you afraid of? Are your fears real? Are your concerns serving you?

4. Set a game plan to get to where you want to go. What other resources do you need? What do you need to learn about? What

things do you need? Who can you get help from to get you where you want to go?

5. Set goals on a timeline. What can you do tomorrow? Next week? Next month? Next year?

6. It is always best to work with someone you respect and trust—someone who will help support you and give you feedback, a different perspective, and advice. It can be a life coach, close friend, or family member.

7. Go for it!

CHAPTER ELEVEN

Gratitude

"To educate yourself for the feeling of gratitude means to take nothing for granted, but to always seek out and value the kind that will stand behind the action. Nothing that is done for you is a matter of course. Everything originates in a will for the good, which is directed at you. Train yourself to never put off the word or action for the expression of gratitude."

—Albert Schweitzer

"Remember, not getting what you want is sometimes a great stroke of luck."

—Dalai Lama

"Gratitude goes hand in hand with love, and where one is, the other must be found. For gratitude is but an aspect of the Love which is the Source of all creation."

—A Course in Miracles, Lesson 195

"There are many in the world who are dying for a piece of bread, but there are many more dying for a little love."

—Mother Teresa

"Gratitude is not only the greatest of virtues, but the parent of all others."

—Cicero

I n her book, *7 Course Meal For the Soul,* Angi Covington wrote,
If the world's population were reduced to a village of one hundred people,
there would be:

- Fifty-seven Asians
- Twenty-one Europeans
- Fourteen Americans (North, Central, and South)
- Eight Africans

These would further be divided in the following ways:

- Six people would possess 59% of the wealth, and they would all be from the United States. Eighty people would live in poverty.
- One would be dying, and one would be born.
- Seventy would be illiterate.
- One would have a university degree.
- Fifty would suffer from hunger and malnutrition.
- If you had a full refrigerator, a roof over your head, clothes, and a place to sleep, you would have it better than 75% of people.
- If you had money in the bank, in your wallet, or in your pocket or purse, you would be the privileged top 12% of the 100 people.
- If you woke up healthy, you would have it better than one million people, who won't live through the week.

When I stopped working full-time in Chico, California, I continued to do part-time work at a pain clinic just to make ends meet and to pay bills. During the Christmas holidays in 2008, there was a general sense of anxiety and depression. It was the time of the economic meltdown, and many of my patients were having financial difficulties. Many had lost their jobs and couldn't find a new one. Some were having difficulty paying their mortgage and were at risk of losing their homes. Most didn't have the money to buy Christmas presents. Oftentimes, the holidays bring feelings of sadness over loss of loved ones through death or estrangement. Other times, people are depressed during Christmas because their lives are not what they thought they would be like when they were younger and hopeful with expectations of life. Through the department store commercials and advertisements, Christmas has come to represent consumerism. It has come to equate "things" with love.

Christmas has become based on the wants for self and for others. Earlier in my life, I remember Christmas morning as high-energy: a "feeding frenzy" of ripping open presents. That frenzy would last until mid-morning when suddenly, with all the presents opened, there would be an emptiness—a deflation of energy—and the excitement would be gone.

I reminded my patients that the purpose of Christmas was to celebrate the birth of Jesus Christ and the reason he came to the world. Jesus came to the world for the salvation of mankind from pain and suffering. Salvation comes from unconditional love. Buddha taught of enlightenment (ultimate truth), but enlightenment is rare and very hard to achieve. Love, however, is something that is achievable by most anyone who wishes to pursue it. I have lived over half a century, and it wasn't until recently that I realized that love and gratitude are the same thing. When you love someone or something (like a place or experience), you place great value on them and have gratitude for them. As opposed to *wanting*, gratitude is about *having*. You can't have gratitude for what you want.

The true meaning of Christmas is about having gratitude for what you have, instead of what you want. It is about the presence (with a "ce") of what you have in your life now, instead of the presents (with an "ts") of what you want.

I was inspired to send a personal "thank you" to all those people in my life for being in my life and to tell them how much they meant to me. In the spirit of Christmas, I advised the patients I saw in clinic to appreciate what they had, instead of focusing on what they didn't have and what they wanted. It doesn't cost much to tell others how grateful you are for having friends, family, and loved ones in your life. It doesn't cost much to say "thank you."

The Health Benefits of Gratitude

Expressing gratitude initiates a powerful healing effect in your own mind and body. Robert Emmons at University of California, Davis and Michael McCullough at the University of Miami were co-investigaors research has shown that gratitude makes people happier, healthier, and more optimistic (Emmons and McCullough, 2003). It also improves sleep (Wood and Lloyd, 2009). It has also been shown that living in gratitude eliminates obstacles that prevent you from reaching your goals in life. Gratitude makes you more alert, enthusiastic, and better able to handle stress.

Dr. Emmons performed studies demonstrating that individuals with gratitude had a heightened sense of well-being relative to control groups. They also included studies of people with neuromuscular disease. Gratitude was found to help with mood, coping behaviors, physical symptoms, and outlook on life. The greater the gratitude, the greater the health benefits.

Gratitude not only helps improve our sense of well-being; it also improves the well-being of our relationships with others. It shifts perspectives and allows us to see the good in others. Many people looking for happiness in their lives are looking for "things" to make them happy—things outside themselves. We all live in hope that the next thing will make us happy, but it just creates unhappiness, because that "thing" may not be obtainable, or that "thing" can be taken away.

Having greater gratitude is directly related to greater happiness. In a study performed at Leicester University in England (as reported on *60 Minutes* on 6/12/08), Denmark was ranked as the happiest country in the world. The US, however, ranked twenty-third. The people of Denmark demonstrate a low level of expectation and sense of entitlement. They demonstrated humility and gratitude for anything. The Danes reported more interest in relationships than in material possessions, in contrast to the consumerism in the United States. Interestingly, the United States ranks twenty-third in health, as well. Perhaps this suggests a direct correlation between happiness and health.

How often do we take so many of our life's gifts for granted: to breathe, to witness a beautiful sunset, to hear inspiring music, to smell fresh-cut flowers, to taste an exquisite meal, to touch the hand of a loved one, to walk and dance, to experience love and joy? How easy is it to take the things in life for granted—without gratitude—until those things are taken away? It is impossible to live in grief of loss and gratitude at the same time.

Gratitude is the appreciation of something greater than the self. Gratitude is first taught at birth, with mother-child bonding. Upon seeing her newborn baby, the mother suddenly has a change in brain pattern to overcome instinctual self-preservation. She develops a willingness to sacrifice her own life for that of another. The infant develops gratitude from the mother's love. One person gives love, and love is returned in the form of gratitude. Gratitude is supportive of life. Numerous social and scientific studies show that infants who don't receive love from birth to three years of age develop more health and psychological diseases than those who receive maternal love. They also die earlier.

How many people have gratitude for being able to experience pain? Almost all people don't want to experience pain and suffering. Most say their lives would be so much better if they didn't experience pain. Pain acts as an alarm that something is wrong with the body. Leprosy is a disease that has been known since Biblical times. It is caused by a microorganism that attacks nerves, affecting sensation and muscle strength. Without sensation, the body will be unaware if it has a decayed tooth or if you step on a nail. As a result, infections are allowed to progress, leading to skin sores, disfigurement, and amputations.

People with disease tend to vilify the part of the body that is causing suffering and try to separate themselves from that part of their body. They fight against themselves, which can contribute to autoimmune disease. There was an elderly woman I saw as a patient who suffered Crohn's disease (an inflammatory disease of the intestine). She confessed that she had been raped by a family member when she was a child and had suffered shame in silence. There was another woman who suffered from pelvic pain from chronic cystitis (bladder inflammation) who practiced infidelity in response to her husband's infidelity and had suppressed anger. Many diseases are wars with the self and are associated with subconscious guilt or subconscious blame and resentment.

We declare war on so many things in life that we don't want (i.e., the wars on drugs, against terrorism, on cancer, etc.). I have talked to numerous individuals who were able to recover from otherwise terminal diseases, and it wasn't until they were able to understand and make peace with their condition that they were able to heal. Many actually expressed gratitude for the disease's message that they needed to change their attitude about life and their lifestyle. Having gratitude does not mean surrendering passively to the disease out of hopelessness. It means having an understanding of what is happening and an appreciation for the cause and meaning behind the disease. Healing means overcoming the fear of what the illness might mean and working with healing the condition from a physical (i.e., medications and treatments), mental and emotional (i.e., the beliefs and thought patterns that create disease or prevent healing), and spiritual approach (i.e., the willingness to surrender one's self-righteousness and open up the consciousness to a greater understanding).

There are times when pain is created as a symbol of something else. An orthopedic surgeon referred a man to me who was experiencing continued shoulder-and-arm pain, despite what had been an otherwise successful shoulder surgery. The man had failed all conventional medical treatment for his arm pain. I diagnosed him with a condition called complex regional pain syndrome. When I examined him, he had a tattoo of a name on his shoulder. The name belonged to his son, who had died twelve years earlier in an auto accident. The man said his heart had lost all energy to live, and he had developed multiple medical problems after his son's death. It was no wonder he continued to have pain in his shoulder after surgery. The man was symbolically "shouldering" the grief for his son where the boy's name was tattooed.

It is human nature to resist things we don't want. At all levels in animal survival, the distinctions are made between what is desired and what is to be avoided. The desire to escape something painful is a primitive reflex. When you touch something hot, step on something sharp, or see something that makes you afraid, the natural tendency is to withdraw from the cause of the pain or discomfort. Conscious resistance through denial of the fight-or-flight reflex causes stress. In our society, we are in a state of chronic stress, which perpetuates the physiologic changes and leads to diseases—both physical and mental. We make ourselves stay in unhappy relationships or work jobs we hate. Much of the stress can often be related to anger, guilt, or shame over something that happened in the past, or we fear or worry about the possibilities of the future.

As discussed in a previous chapter, the power of thought (i.e., focusing all our attention on what we don't want) paradoxically strengthens that thought and condition. Resisting something makes it stronger. Put another way, that which you resist, persists. We are fighting against ourselves. Any effort to fight meets a matching resistance to maintain the conflict. By accepting the condition and not resisting it, the conflict and associated stress resolve.

Viktor Frankl created a psychological technique called logotherapy, in which permission is given to perform the act being repressed, thereby extinguishing further rumination of the thought. An example is a young doctor who would sweat profusely when speaking in public. The more he tried to resist sweating, the greater the anxiety and the worst the sweating would become before and during the public speaking event. Dr. Frankl treated the patient by telling him to attempt to sweat as much as he could before the public speaking event. As hard as the young doctor tried to sweat, he couldn't, and therefore, he became cured. How often do we try to suppress a laugh, and it just keeps building until it can no longer be contained? There are patients I treat who become sick with worry. "Do you know what is wrong with you?" I ask them. "You don't worry enough. You need to worry twenty-four hours a day for the next week without taking a break." I would follow up after a week, and the worry would be gone.

I use the analogy of our mind and body being like a house with the doors and windows open. An emotion or pain will come through like a wind. Once the wind starts whistling through the house, the natural tendency is to resist the wind and close the doors and windows. Unfortunately, once trapped in the house, the wind has no place to go and will damage the house. Like the wind, pain and suffering are temporary. They come, and they go. They will not stay forever—unless we resist them.

One of my teachers, Tim Hallbom, told of a friend who never got depressed. Being curious, Tim eventually asked him why he never got depressed. "When I was a child," he said, "if I didn't study and did poorly on a test—or if I left my bicycle in the driveway, and my father ran over my bike coming home from work—my parents never said to me, 'That was stupid,' or, 'You were bad for doing that.' They never put judgment on the event. Instead, they would say, 'What did you learn from that? What was the lesson you learned from that event?' So, things were either good, or they were lessons."

Viewing events with blame or judgment leads to unhappiness. Friends give support. Enemies give lessons. You choose to label something as good or bad with gratitude or resentment. It is easy to reflect on and remember all the pleasant things in life. It is more difficult to changed perceived "bad" into life lessons and have gratitude for those, as well. Acceptance equals forgiveness, which leads to gratitude and happiness.

It is the mind and our own self-righteousness that keep us where we are—whether it be in pain or in suffering. When we develop a greater understanding in acceptance without being right or wrong, it leads to acceptance and transcendence. By having gratitude for the lessons learned, we become healthier and less resentful.

Not living in the present just leads to suffering. What we have in the present is all we have: no more and no less. The present is the only time we have the power to change anything. We can't change the events that happened in the past. Only in the present can we change our attitude toward the past. Attitude plays a large role in gratitude. Enjoying and appreciating what we have right now is the key to being present. Giving thanks is a key component and the power of any prayer. Oftentimes, abundance is ignored and not valued. Nothing that is expected or entitled is appreciated. The well-known phrase "attitude is everything" has great truth behind it. It is a choice of seeing the glass as half-full, instead of half-empty.

Expectations

Gratitude is not comparing oneself or what one has with others. Pride causes one to think one is better or worth more than another, and that is not love. There is a biblical story in Matthew 20:1–16. A land owner goes out early one morning to hire workers to help harvest his field. He and the workers agree on a price, and the workers go into the field. A few hours later, the land owner goes back to the hiring hall and brings back additional workers. Again, at noon and mid-afternoon, he does the same thing. At early evening, the land owner goes into town again and sees more men standing around. He asks them, "Why haven't you been working?"

"Because no one hired us," they reply.

"Then go out to my field with the rest of the workers," the land owner tells them.

At the end of the work day, the land owner tells the paymaster to pay the workers, starting with the last man hired—and to pay each of the workers the same. The workers who were hired early in the morning assumed they would be paid more than the workers who got hired at the end of the day. They become angry when they (who worked a full day) are paid the same as the other workers (who only worked an hour).

"Friends," the land owner responds, "I did you no wrong! I paid you what we agreed upon. Take it and go. It is my desire to pay you all the same. Is it against the law to give away my money if I want to? Should you be angry because I am kind? And so it is that the last should be first and the first, last."

This was a difficult story for me to reconcile at first. How is that fair? A worker gets paid the same for working one hour as another worker who worked the whole day? The workers who worked the whole day compared themselves to the other workers and felt they were entitled to receive more than the others, even though they had been paid what had been agreed upon.

Because of their sense of entitlement and expectation, they felt they deserved more and had no gratitude for what they did receive. They felt they deserved more.

Love and gratitude are the same. Love is not about making comparisons. Some women will look at another woman getting a diamond ring and equate more love with a bigger diamond. A man may see his wife get older and equate her physical attractiveness with her value. How can one, out of gratitude and love, suffer less because one sees another suffer more? When we compare ourselves with others, we see ourselves as separate. Love is valuing others with gratitude. Love is seeing the sameness in another.

A sense of entitlement and expectation causes unhappiness that comes from the ego. When we feel entitled, we never experience gratitude. Living with feelings of entitlement or expectation is not being happy with what we have *now*. Entitlement and expectation are overcome by humility. Humility is the realization of our sphere of control. It is the understanding that we can only truly control ourselves. Trying to control others or blaming others for our unhappiness does nothing but cause more unhappiness. It does nothing to affect the other person or to improve the situation.

There are useful practices to attract what one desires. Setting intention is powerful, but desiring (i.e., wanting it too much) can be an obstacle. In any relationship, the one who desires less has more control over the relationship. With the ego-centric mind, desiring is more consuming than having. Be grateful for what you have. The truth is that the more you own, whether it be things or relationships, the more you are owned. With ownership comes the responsibility to put energy into maintaining what you have—and engenders the fear of losing it.

Often people have a lack of gratitude because of an inner sense of emptiness. They feel that if they just had more "things" or love from others, they would be happier. The truth is that happiness doesn't come from outside themselves, but from the inside.

Sometimes, it isn't until we experience loss that we feel gratitude. People who have had near-death experiences or have survived terminal diseases live with gratitude for their lives. Think of your body as your best friend. You want what's best for your best friend. You want your friend to be healthy and strong. If your best friend is sick, you don't get mad and hate your friend. You give love and chicken soup. Like a good friend, you can tell your body how much you love it and how grateful you are for having it in your life. By giving love, you make your body feel better and healthier. It will make you feel better about yourself. Gratitude is the exchange of life energy; it energizes you. It has the greatest effect on improving the body's vital signs. The paradox is that by thinking about what you lack, you never feel fulfilled You don't enhance your life by feeling sorry for yourself. You must develop love for yourself—not so much for what you have, but for what you are. The more grateful you are, the more love you receive in your life.

Exercise

1. "You rock!" This has become something of a family ritual for us. Dinner time is when we all sit around the table and share the events of the day. The ritual involves each person at the table saying something for which they are grateful about the other people at the table. We say, "You rock because …" We then move on to the next person, until everyone has been included. Then it is the next person's turn to do the same thing, until everyone has had a turn of giving and receiving gratitude from every person there.

2. What is something you learned today that you are grateful for? This is an opportunity to change the day's negative events into positive events. It can reflect life lessons that are not be repeated.

Wake up every morning saying: 1.) "I am grateful for being alive"; 2.) "I am grateful for the things I have"; and 3.) "I am grateful for the things I will do today." Keep it simple. You might include only two or three things under each item. Show an act of kindness for someone else without expecting acknowledgement or applause. Do something nice for yourself today to honor yourself and your life.

CHAPTER TWELVE

Humor

"[W]ith humor, the equation is tragedy plus time equals comedy. I am just at tragedy right now."

—Tig Notaro

"Comedy is the art of telling the truth about being human. The truth is: We all have flaws."

—Steven Kaplan

"Sometimes, I lie awake at night and ask, 'Where have I gone wrong?' Then a voice says to me, 'This is going to take more than one night.'"

—Charles M. Schultz

"Humor is mankind's greatest blessing."

—Mark Twain

"It's a dog-eat-dog world, Woody, and I'm wearing Milk Bone underwear."

—Norm Peterson, from Cheers

"Love is an attachment to another self. Humor is a form of self-detachment: a way of looking at one's existence, one's misfortune, or one's discomfort. If you really love, if you really know how to laugh, the result is the same: You forget yourself."

—Claude Roy

Domestic violence is one of the most dangerous calls a police officer can take. I heard a story about a policewoman responding to a domestic violence call. As she walked up to the apartment, she could hear loud screaming coming from an upstairs unit. As she started to climb the stairs, she heard a scream and the sound of shattering glass as a television was thrown out of the apartment front window, smashing into the ground below. Nervously, she knocked on the door.

"What the !@#$ do you want?" shouted an angry male voice at her through the door.

"TV repairman," she replied.

There was a sudden moment of silence in the apartment, and the man opened the door in a much calmer state. The policewoman was able to diffuse the dangerous conflict with the use of humor. Emotional states such as fear, depression or anger can be disarmed with the use of humor.

Over 2,500 years ago in ancient Greek plays, the theme was either that of tragedy or humor. The paradox is that life can be a place of heaven or hell, genius or insanity, and humor or tragedy. There is a saying: "The distance between genius and insanity is measured by success." Success is accomplishing an aim or purpose. Humor has the power to turn any defeat into a success. Successful people in life are able to direct their focus to the positive by minimizing the severity of any tragedy. The humor or tragedy can be seen in the same event when observed from different perspectives. All of us have bad things happen in life. The ability to find humor helps us take life's punches and not get knocked down.

Comedians have used humor as a way to escape traumatic childhoods. Tragedy and crisis breed creativity. Many comedians, like Charlie Chaplin, overcame childhood tragedy and abuse through comedy. Humor is a way to detach emotionally from a painful situation and allow a more neutral perspective. A sense of humor improves a person's ability to overcome disappointment and adversity. Comedy is about not taking life or yourself too seriously. It teaches one to have more humility about life.

Humor and Health

Studies on animals and humans have shown that stress increases cardiovascular disease, leads to hypertension, impairs protective killer cells

(Segerstrom S. 2004) and causes premature aging and death. Joel E Demsdale writes in his 2008 State-of-of-the-Art paper (JACC Journal Vol. 51, Issue 13, April 2008), "…the overall data suggest that stress contributes to adverse clinical cardiac events and provides a milieu of increased vulnerability to the heart." Chronic stress increases the brain release of ACTH molecules that increase the blood level of corticosteroids ten fold (Young and Akil 1985). Increased corticosteroids leads to elevated blood pressure, upper body fat, acne, muscle and bone weakness. Scientists have been interested in the causes for aging and diseases, such as cancer. The ability to reproduce healthy cells is dependent on healthy DNA. We discussed telomeres in the chapter on stress and disease. Stress affects these telomeres, causing mutations like cancer and premature cell death. Compassion and humor are thought to have an effect on lengthening telomeres, making our genes more stable.

Research has shown that humor has a significant effect on the mind, providing a greater sense of well-being. Humor also affects healing from some physical diseases, decreases pain from chronic disease, and improves the body's immune response. Laughter has been shown to decrease serum cortisol levels, decrease sympathetic tone, and increase parasympathetic tone, which are factors that slow aging and improve health.

Researcher Lee Berk, an Associate Professor at Loma Linda University in California showed comedy tapes to test subjects who were hooked up to IVs, and every ten minutes, he took blood samples. He found levels of stress hormones, cortisol, and epinephrine to be lower when the test subjects laughed. In addition, he discovered immune antibody "A" levels increased with laughter, which helps both white blood cells and killer cells fight upper respiratory infections. Laughter also has been shown to decrease nausea and improve appetite in patients receiving chemotherapy. Laughter affects the musculoskeletal system, relaxing muscles and decreasing muscle tone for up to forty-five minutes. It has been shown that humor and laughter can decrease the use of pain medication during and after painful medical and surgical procedures.

Humor can not only empower one to get emotional distance from troublesome issues; we can actually distance ourselves from our illness and disease, as well. This was the belief of Norman Cousins, who became interested in the affect of emotions on our health. He was a writer and eventual editor for the *Saturday Review* who developed several illnesses, including heart disease and a musculoskeletal disorder called ankylosing spondylitis: a disease in which the connective tissue in the joints of the spine becomes inflamed and fused, causing extreme pain. His doctors not only told him his condition was terminal, but also gave him a 1-in-500 chance of recovery with conventional medical treatment.

Norman Cousins wanted to take a more active role in his treatment, and with the assistance of physician friends, he began to research other ways of healing. He began to take large quantities of vitamin C. He discharged himself from the hospital because he felt it didn't provide an environment conducive to healing, due to its negative attitude, degree of stress, disrupted sleep patterns, and culture of overmedication. He also reasoned that if negative emotions were known to contribute to illness, then positive emotions should have a positive effect. He decided to use humor and laughter as a means of recovering from his disease.

He checked himself into a hotel room and watched comedy shows, such as *Candid Camera*, along with Marx Brothers movies. Whenever he experienced pain or depression, he watched the films that made him laugh so hard his stomach ached. The pain was worse at night, and he found that laughter allowed him more hours of sleep. Laughter and humor changed his brain and body chemistry. Laboratory tests demonstrated that with laughter, his blood sedimentation rate improved. He was able to get off almost all of his medication. He found that ten minutes of solid laughter gave him two hours of pain-free sleep. Norman Cousins eventually recovered and became affiliated with UCLA Medical School as an adjunct professor. He wrote about his personal experiences regarding the power of humor in healing in his book *Anatomy of Illness as Perceived By a Patient*, which later became a movie.

Humor and Brain Function

The brain can become imprisoned by negative emotions such as pride, anger, fear, guilt, or shame. Negative emotions narrow one's mental focus and impair reason and problem-solving. Decisions based on fear and anger are oftentimes the wrong decision. Humor allows for a shift in perspective to escape the emotional prison, allowing one to look at the situation from a different perspective.

Humor has a positive affect on brain function by stimulating different parts of the brain.

Humor has been shown to:

1.   increase activity in the right prefrontal cortex;

2.   increase creativity;

3.   increase socialization judgment; and

4.   improve memory.

The prefrontal cortex is the region of the brain stimulated by humor. Damage to this area affects a person's ability to understand and laugh at jokes. The right prefrontal cortex is the region of the brain associated with empathy and compassion, allowing one to better relate to others. Allan L. Reiss and his associates at Stanford (Mobbs and Hagan, 2005) were able to discern the effects of humor on introverted versus extroverted personality types and the response of the areas of the brain to humor. Extroverts tend to activate the prefrontal cortex and surrounding area. Introverts activate the amygdala and parts of the temporal lobe (see Appendix A for more on brain pathways). With depression and stress, the brain gets stuck in the left hemisphere, running its circuits like a dog chasing its tail with no chance of escape. Scientists have discovered that humor activates both left and right hemispheres of the brain. In his book *Emotional Intelligence*, Daniel Goleman notes, "Laughter seems to help people think more broadly and associate more freely."

David Abrambis at California State University at Long Beach found that people who use humor and are playful on the job are more creative and productive, get along better with co- workers, are better decision-makers, and have a lower rate of absenteeism and sick days. It is known that creativity and humor enhances and sustains life.

Psychologists have found that when you are able to make others laugh with you, you gain greater rapport. After a laugh, others are likely to be more receptive to your message—even if it is something they don't want to hear. Humor is a way to get around another person's defensiveness. Research has also shown that having a sense of humor makes one more attractive to others. People just naturally want to be around others who are happy and more joyful. Humor brings joy into life that nourishes life.

In a 2007 *Reader's Digest* article, the qualities of a comedian were listed as integrity, vulnerability, and not wanting to seek the approval of others. As humans, we all experience similar feelings of depression, anger, or love. It is the ability and courage to connect with our own feelings out of integrity that enables us to connect with others. Use of humor is the willingness to be open to exploring our own emotions and the willingness to look at a traumatic situation in a healthier way. Vulnerability is to surrender our defenses and look at ourselves with honesty. Everyone has a dark side. It is the acknowledgment of our own frailties that allows us to connect with others who have the same frailties. So often, we don't want to expose our weakness because of shame and the fear of being judged. It's difficult, if not impossible, to be funny when one is worried about what other people think. Humor requires one to think outside the box.

Types of Humor

In ancient Greece, Plato wrote of the superiority theory of humor: We laugh when we see someone else in an embarrassing or undignified situation as an expression of our superiority over the embarrassed individual. That embarrassed individual can be ourselves. By looking back and finding humor in painful or traumatic experiences from our past, we can emotionally distance ourselves, show superiority over our former selves, and take pride on how far we have come in the present.

Primitive humor makes fun of other people to feel better about ourselves. If you are a recipient of primitive humor, find some ways to overcome insult with humor. An example of this is a story about Winston Churchill. Winston Churchill had been confronted by a hostile Lady Nancy Astor, who told him that if he were her husband, she would poison his tea. The quick-witted Churchill replied, "Nancy, if I were your husband, I would drink it."

The best humor is self-deprecating. If one can make fun of oneself, it takes the power away from what anyone else might say. This type of humor also is less offensive than making fun of others. Humor is supposed to make people feel good, not embarrassed, insulted, or offended. Tom Antion, a humor consultant, says, "Telling funny stories on yourself creates an impression that you're secure, confident, and likable. ... Weak people feel the need to inflate themselves; confident people don't."

Humor can also nurture relationships. People want to feel good, and they want to be around people that make them feel good. Our emotions connect us in our relationships. In the right setting, humor can be used to lift a friend who is depressed or angry, changing the state of their feelings.

One of the steps to finding humor is letting the inner child out to play. Hunter "Patch" Adams was a medical student at the Medical College of Virginia in 1971. He was convinced about the powerful connection between health and the environment. He believed that individual health could not be separated from the health of the family, community, and world. His healing techniques were not appreciated by his medical school teachers. With his unorthodox techniques, however, he was able to assist in healing patients to a greater degree than his colleagues, who used evidence-based, traditional medical treatment. His prescription for healing included patient and staff participation in play and laughter. "Patch" Adams started the Gesundheit! Institute in West Virginia as an adjunct to conventional medical treatment. The institute uses play and humor, as well as alternative healing techniques such as acupuncture, homeopathy, performing arts, crafts, recreation, and nature. His story was also made into a movie with Robin Williams, called *Patch Adams.*

My Not-So-Funny Comedy Experience

The TV program *Whose Line Is It Anyway?* was an improvisational comedy show consisting of a panel of four performers who created characters, scenes, and songs on the spot. Many of the skits and short routines were hilarious, and it fascinated me how the performers are able to spontaneously create their material. It demonstrated the connection between humor and creativity.

"Laughter is the best medicine." I have always heard that saying but didn't know how to apply it. I wanted to find out if someone could be taught to use comedy to pull themselves out of tragedy. I decided to fly down to Hollywood, California, and participate in an improvisational comedy training program called *Second City. Second City* was the birthplace of the careers of some of the best-known comedians, including John Belushi, Bill Murray, John Candy, Mike Meyers, Julia Louis-Dreyfus, and Dan Aykroyd, to name just a few. I wanted to find out if there was a magic formula to humor. I wanted to find a way to teach it to patients to help them recontextualize traumatic events in their lives in order to help overcome them. Those attending the class included actresses, stand-up comedians, drama students from UCLA … Then there was me. Graduation from the class involved performing live in a night club setting with an audience. It was truly out of my comfort zone. I was totally overwhelmed and a nervous wreck. Out of all the classes I'd taken throughout my career, this one was the hardest and most intimidating.

In all honesty, I have to admit that I really sucked at my performance. When I made a joke, there would be dead silence in the audience. It was not like the cartoons I used to watch in which, after a character performed, there would be no audience applause, and all that could be heard was the sound of chirping crickets. After my act, there were no crickets. After seeing my performance, the crickets were all at the admission window in front of the theater, trying to get their money back. Needless to say, I'm still a comedy work in progress. As humiliating of an experience as performing in the comedy club was for me, the benefit was in finding courage to walk through my fear.

Humor Is a Choice

There is a common misconception that humor is something people are just naturally born with. It is true that there are people who are born with comedic gifts. That doesn't mean, however, that humor can't be learned or taught. A person can love basketball and practice the sport, but that doesn't mean he will be another Michael Jordan. Success in humor doesn't mean you will have your own sitcom; you can, however, look at your life as your personal sitcom, in which you are the writer and director. You can choose to write your life as a tragedy or as a comedy. You can practice and work on humor to be successful in finding the joy in life that humor brings.

How we want to live our lives is a choice. We can choose to live in despair and helplessness, or we can choose to turn our lives around to be happier. The easiest thing to do is to just give up. Nobody else can pull us out of tragedy. As mentioned throughout this book, making a commitment to change our attitude will transcend our personal hell into heaven.

We have discussed the false power of being a victim. Victims live in a world of anger, shame, and pride. Humor provides a way out of those negative emotional energies. Some people might say that they can't find the humor. If they are totally honest, they really don't *want* to find the humor. They would rather take pride in being a victim who has been wronged. Pride is the most powerful egoic emotion, but it is also the most stubborn. Pride is self-righteousness and thinking, "My way is the only right way." It prevents, however, a person from exploring other possibilities that might be better. The antidotes for pride are humor and humility.

A person can assume one of two roles: either the hero or the comedian. As heroes, some people have the strength, courage, and tools to pull themselves out of a predicament. Assuming the role of hero, however, is also stressful. It means having to be a perfectionist, having all the answers, and not being allowed to fail. A hero lives in pride and doesn't think he or she has any flaws, even though the flaws are there for everyone else to see.

For the rest of us, there is humor. In his book *Hidden Tools of Comedy*, Steven Kaplan defines the comedic character as a "non-hero." He writes, "A 'non-hero' is an ordinary guy or gal struggling against insurmountable odds without many of the required skills and tools with which to win, yet never giving up hope." We can beat ourselves up for not being a hero or not being perfect, or we can be more realistic and accept—and even embrace—our imperfections and flaws. That's what makes for good comedy.

In comedy, our flaws are our tools. No one is perfect, and comedy gives us permission to be human. If a hero doesn't achieve success, it is a tragedy. If a non-hero doesn't achieve success, it is comedy. When we are able to share our flaws in a humorous way, it creates better rapport with others and with ourselves. By opening ourselves up and exposing our flaws in a humorous way, we are more accessible to others. When we let our guard down, we allow others to come in.

How does one find humor in life? First, it is about attitude. You have to decide that you are going to focus on being funny. You can't be funny unless you *choose* to be funny. What does "being funny" look like, sound like, and feel like for you? Humor is such a subjective thing. What may be funny to one person will be considered offensive to another. Some people like slap-stick humor (e.g., The Three Stooges), and others like situational comedy (e.g., *Seinfeld*). Think about events and memories in your life that were funny. Think about your favorite comedian or sit-com. What I found to be helpful was to watch or listen to comedy programs that I considered funny. This put me in the mood to create my own humor.

Every day, focus on finding funny things that happen in your life. When you set the intention of finding funny things, you become more perceptive to funny things around you. It is like buying a new brand of car, like a Subaru Outback. Suddenly, you start to see all the other Subaru Outbacks out on the streets that you wouldn't have seen before you bought one. If you can't find something funny, make something up that would be funny.

Second, direct humor at your own frailties. Sharing our own life embarrassments in a humorous way creates rapport with others. The humor doesn't have to be done out of self-humiliation or self-deprecation. Be yourself, and be genuine in your humor. Humor allows you to be impervious to attack. When a hero is attacked, he has to defend his weaknesses and flaws. It leads to fear and anger. The comedian, who already knows his flaws and accepts them with humor, is impervious to attack.

Third, if you are involved in a tragedy, it takes time to let the grief or anger run its course before trying to change your emotions. Some have said that time is the best healer. Besides time, becoming the witness/observer allows you to gain a different perspective on the situation. Sometimes, you identify with your feelings and emotions so much that they it becomes overwhelming. You become trapped by those feelings and unable to find the humor in the situation. A tool you can use is to make a picture of yourself outside of yourself, with whomever else is there in the tragedy. The further you are able to move the picture away from *you*, the smaller the picture becomes and the weaker the negative feelings. By distancing the picture of yourself from the situation in your mind, you can gain a different perspective of the situation to find the humor—and to escape.

The paradox of life is that something that is considered tragic can also be humorous. It is about choosing to shift focus. Instead of looking for the negative, look for any positive—no matter how small—to work with, then magnify it. Humor occurs when the ending or conclusion is different than what was anticipated.

How to Create a Joke

Most of us have said something funny at some time in our lives that brought a smile or laugh to someone else. Breaking down humor, however, to teach someone how to be funny requires extensive research. Greg Dean's book *Step by Step to Stand-up Comedy* teaches that the basics of joke structure includes two parts: setup and punch. "The setup is the first part of the joke that sets up the laugh. The punch is the second part that makes you laugh." Humor is created from the paradox of the setup and punch. The setup and punch each give a juxtaposed perspective of the same topic that causes humor. The setup involves a theme that leads the listener down a road of expectation, and the punch provides a short, surprise detour that leads to humor. Greg Dean writes, "The trick is you cannot be surprised [punch] unless you're expecting something else first [setup]. That's what a joke does."

It's like saying sadly, "My wife just ran off with my best friend ... Boy, do I miss him."

Allen Klein became interested in the use of humor in improving health, and his research produced his book *The Healing Power of Humor*. In the book, Klein gives tools to people that allow them to transcend their emotional and physical pain. He talks about using humor appropriately to not only get others out of pain but also oneself.

Among the tools Klein uses for humor are *exaggeration, nonsense,* and *word play.*

1. *Exaggeration* can be an over-estimation of one's ability or frailties. Think of Woody Allen, who magnifies his neurosis, which creates humor.

    - Rodney Dangerfield would "get no respect": "When I was a baby, my mom wouldn't breastfeed me. She just wanted to be friends." Or, "When I was a child, the pets wouldn't give me any respect. I would play in the sandbox, and the cat kept trying to cover me up."

2. *Nonsense* can be used to diffuse an emotional upset through absurdity. The police woman calling herself a TV repairman at the beginning of the chapter is an example.

    - I love Steve Martin's "wild and crazy guy" humor in this regard. He makes fun of himself by calling himself a "swinging sex god": "Many people come to me and ask me, 'How can you be such a 'swinging sex god.' I like to be a unique guy that has his own special scent. Not to smell like every other guy. I like to have my own individual aroma. That's why I wear a tuna fish sandwich. I put a tuna fish sandwich under each arm, maybe one or two behind each ear. I don't smell like any other guy. And it's economical, too, because the smell lasts for four or five days."

- Another example occurred while I was working on this chapter. I took my mother to be admitted to the hospital for hip replacement surgery. She made a mistake, however, and stopped her heart medication a week before her scheduled surgery. Because of this, her surgery had to be postponed for a later date. She was very distraught on the car ride back home, but we decided to go out for Chinese food for lunch. She had had to stop eating the night before her surgery, so she was hungry. Using humor to get her out of her funk, I told her, "Oh, I get it mom. But you didn't have to sabotage your surgery just to have me take you out for lunch." We both started to laugh, and her mood lifted.

3. *Word play* can be done in two different ways. Word play can be substituting the same word, giving it another meaning, or it can be using a humorous metaphor for the word or situation.

- An example of the first illustration is the joke about a man walking into the doctor's office dressed in nothing but transparent plastic food wrap. The doctor takes one look at him and says, "I see what your problem is … I can see your/you're nuts!" The word *nuts* gets moved from one context into another totally different context, which creates humor.
- An example of the second use of *word play* involves using another word or phrase to describe a situation. Jerry Seinfeld is a master of this technique. In one of the episodes of his television show, *Seinfeld*, Elaine used a sponge contraceptive, and throughout the episode, she was looking for a boyfriend who was "sponge-worthy." In another episode, the friends had a contest to see who could remain celibate the longest: to be "master of my domain."
- David Letterman used word play in his "Top Ten" lists. His "Top 10 Polite Ways To Say 'Your Zipper Is Down' " include the examples:

- "The cucumber has left the salad."
- "You need to bring your tray table into the upright and locked position."
- "Elvis has left the building."
- "You've got a security breach at Los Pantalones."
- "Men are from Mars ... but I see something that rhymes with Venus."

"That's the Saddest Story I've Ever Heard!"

When you find there is no one else who wants to listen to your sad story, the following is an exercise you can do by yourself. Write the words "that's the saddest story I've ever heard!" on a Post-it or piece of paper, then tape it to a mirror. Tell your sad story to yourself in the mirror. Every once in a while, look at the note. To make the experience even more powerful, put on a funny prop (like a clown nose or funny glasses) while you are telling your sad story. When you look in the mirror with the props and tell your story, you take your story less seriously and are better able to move on in your life.

Humor and the Inner Critic

I have one of the most aggressive and unrelenting inner critics ever. My inner critic has the power to make me withdraw in shame, guilt, or fear. When the inner critic attacks, I have to resist or defend with anger. Unfortunately, how do we defend ourselves against something that is in our mind?

The inner critic is not who we are, but comes from the beliefs of a previous authority figure, like a teacher, older sibling, or parent. The authority says or does something that was interpreted in a more personal way. The inner critic is able to make us feel bad about ourselves because part of us believes the criticism. The inner critic comes in different forms. It can be the perfectionist or comparer, telling you that nothing you do is good enough or that you're not as good as others. The inner critic can make you responsible for what other people think or do. It can make you feel unworthy or undeserved. It lowers our self-esteem, takes away our power, and leads to unhappiness. It makes us sick.

Our inner critic talks in absolutes. It uses words like *always* or never without being specific: "You *never* do anything right," or, "You're *always* messing up." Absolute words are never true in *all* cases. It leads to the belief that things can't ever change. It makes the situation feel overwhelming. Ask the inner critic for specifics by asking questions. "Always?" "Never?" "Like what or when?" Think about times when it wasn't true—not only for you but for others. By breaking down the attack of absolutes into exactly when it is or isn't true (and under what circumstances), the inner critic becomes easier to deal with.

The inner critic cannot be defeated with resistance or attack; it can only be overcome with understanding. Stacey Sargent's book *Inner Critic Inner Success* describes how we can use our inner critic to become more productive.

1. Get a clearer picture of the critic. What does the critic look like and sound like? Does the inner critic look like anyone you know? What is the inner critic feeling? You can even give the critic a nickname.

2. Identify your emotions associated with the critic: angry, sad, or afraid. You can ask yourself why you feel that way.

3. Identify the top three or four most repetitive, emotionally painful criticisms to work with. Ask yourself if the criticism is 100% true. Is there a truth that is even greater? What else could be true? The inner critic has power over you *only* if you think it is telling the truth.

4. Identify the triggers that bring out the inner critic. Is it a person or situation?

5. Identify the physical reaction: sweaty palms, a knot in the stomach, feeling overwhelmed, etc.

By breaking the inner critic down, it becomes less overwhelming and can be better dealt with. The more you know about your inner critic—and your response to it—the easier it is to change the meaning of the message or focus on observing your physical response and dissociating it from the criticism. You become less of a victim of the inner critic and more proactive in the way you feel. Over time, by reducing the negative emotional reaction, asking questions, and getting a clearer picture of the positive intention for the criticism, you will find a better message or action. Sometimes, however, the anger or guilt is so deep that it is harder to let go. That is when I think about using humor.

During his or her performance, a comedian has to learn to deal with hecklers. Our inner critic is our inner heckler. It looks to demean and demoralize us. Like a heckler, humor can disarm the inner critic by taking the focus off oneself and putting it back on the inner critic. It can shift one's consciousness from self-destruction to the healing emotions of acceptance and joy.

Humor takes you out of a position of being attacked by an inner or outer critic. It can disarm an opponent through confusion and misdirection to give you the advantage. Humor is a form of psychological martial arts. When you practice it, you can be impervious to attack. Humor can turn an opponent's force against himself or herself. Like the movie *Star Wars,* humor is the "force." It should only be used for defense—never for attack. Humor should never be sarcastic or condescending toward another, even the inner critic. I've told my inner critic to "shut up" or "go away," but that doesn't last very long. The inner critic is energized by anger and pride. The antidote to disarming the inner critic with humor is humility. Humility is realizing that no one is perfect. Humility breaks through our pride. When we are in a state of humility, we can't take ourselves, the inner critic, or another antagonizing person too seriously.

Humility is not the same as humiliation. Humiliation is self-belittlement, victimization, and feeling inadequate and powerless. Humility is about feeling adequate, secure, and OK about not being perfect—or feeling special. It is ironic that pride can be attacked, but humility is impervious to attack.

Using humor is like emotional martial arts; it allows us emotional freedom from attack. Like any martial art, it takes practice and training. It means to break the habits or old patterns of allowing criticism to make us feel bad about ourselves. When we feel bad about ourselves, it makes it harder to think and be creative. We can block the attack before we get hurt. By using humility, we beat the inner critic to the punch by agreeing with the attacker with such exaggeration that it sounds absurd and, as a consequence, funny. By poking fun at ourselves and agreeing with the inner critic, we disarm it. The inner critic may say, "You're always doing something stupid." Your response may be, "Hey, that's great! You're right. I know more about being stupid that anyone I know. I'm probably the greatest expert at being stupid. I'm writing a book,

How To Be Stupid for Dummies."

To practice, think of less-intense emotional buttons your inner critic may push, and come up with a funny comeback. When you've mastered lesser opponents, work your way up to more emotionally charged buttons, then come up with funny comebacks for when the inner critic arrives.

If All Else Fails

Finally, if the prior techniques of negotiations and funny comebacks don't work for both the inner or outer critic, just say, "So what?"

Inner critic: "You're stupid!"

You: "So what?"

Inner critic: "You can't do anything right!"

You: "So what?"

There really isn't anything else the inner critic can say. After a while, when the inner critic discovers it can't get to you, it will just leave.

Exercise

Like anything in life, humor takes practice. The more you practice, the faster and easier it comes to you. Keep a journal of humor with funny jokes, experiences, and humorous insights that you can review when feeling down. Write about people or events that commonly drive you crazy, and come up with funny comebacks for future encounters. Writing your own screenplay, identify your hot buttons and the people who push them. Come up with a funny comeback when under attack. You can imagine what your favorite comedian would do in the same situation. What would Woody Allen or Robin Williams do or say? This will prepare you for the next encounter, shifting a painful experience into a humorous one.

Using humor, we escape the emotional cage that traps us in tragedy. Once we are free, we can pursue what we want in life. We can find our life's purpose.

CHAPTER THIRTEEN

Purpose

"The mere possession of a vision is not the same as living it, nor can we encourage others with it if we do not, ourselves, understand and follow its truths. The pattern of the Great Spirit is over us all, but if we follow our own spirits from within, our pattern becomes clearer. For centuries, others have sought their visions. They prepare themselves, so that if the Creator desires them to know their life's purpose, the vision would be revealed. To be blessed with visions is not enough. We must live them!"

—High Eagle

"If you follow your bliss, doors will open where you would have not thought there would be doors and where there wouldn't be a door for anyone else."

—Joseph Campbell

"Life is not easy for any of us. But what is that? We must have perseverance and above all, confidence in ourselves. We must believe that we are gifted for something and that this thing, at whatever cost, must be attained."

—Madam Curie

"This is the true joy in life, being used for a purpose recognized by yourself as a mighty one; the being thoroughly worn out before you are thrown on the scrap heap. Being a force of nature instead of a feverish, selfish little clod of ailments and grievances complaining that the world will not devote itself to making you happy."

—George Bernard Shaw

Man's Search for Meaning

D r. Viktor Frankl was an Austrian neurologist and psychiatrist. He was also Jewish and was imprisoned in the Auschwitz death camp during the time of Nazi Germany. He chronicled his experiences in his book *Man's Search for Meaning*. Being a neurologist and psychiatrist, he provided in his observations a unique perspective into human psychological determinates in surviving life-threatening adversity. The conditions in Auschwitz were so deplorable—with harsh weather and a lack of adequate clothing, food, sanitation, and shelter—that a prisoner would collapse, and within seconds, others would strip his body for his clothes to keep themselves warm. Some prisoners in the camp were so hungry that they resorted to eating their own feces. Prisoners' bodies looked like living skeletons. There were so many dead human bodies that gray, billowy smoke was seen escaping from chimneys of the cremation factories all day and night—and the factories still could not keep up with the number of decaying human carcasses. Many people were sent to the gas chambers for extermination, but the vast majority died of starvation, exposure, disease, and loss of the will to live.

Because of his professional background, Dr. Frankl was able to make clinical observations and determinations of who would survive. Those preoccupied with their own wretched situation and who had a sense of both hopelessness and helplessness very often succumbed and died. Those who lived were able to transcend from their own situation to a greater purpose or higher cause. They wanted to live to see their spouse and children again or to do work that would benefit mankind or the world. Those who died were egocentric and thought only of themselves and their own comfort in self-pity. Those who lived wanted to live in order to give to others or to contribute to a cause greater than themselves.

Purpose and Health

Finding purpose in life is a powerful tool for longevity. In the treatment of post-traumatic stress disorder (PTSD), finding meaning and purpose for the traumatic event is a powerful tool in recovery. We all know of stories of the elderly or terminally ill who are able to continue to live long enough to participate in an important life's accomplishment or event (i.e., a birthday, an anniversary, or the birth of a grandchild). It is unfortunate that we don't really discover what is really important in life until that life is near an end. Those "things" and worries we consider so important in everyday life melt away into insignificance and, eventually, into irrelevance. Suddenly, a revelation of the beauty of life leads to gratitude in the discovery of the true importance of personal relationships. We realize love is the highest value in life. Love provides meaning for our lives that sustains our lives. Many live lives that are unfulfilling and depressing. People commit passive suicide by living in low-vibrational energy levels of apathy, anger, and fear, which leads to greater risk of disease and death. They mask over their unhappiness with addictions and self-destructive behavior. Quite often, people continue to work at a job they hate in order to reach their goal of retirement and think they will be happy to go out and play golf seven days a week. Many eventually do reach their goal of retirement and golfing, but they end up dying within a few years after their retirement. Their goal was met, but their purpose was not life-sustaining. Their meaning and purpose was not directed to contribute to a greater cause beyond their own comfort. A meaningless world engenders fear.

One's life purpose may change throughout a lifetime. At one time, it may be to make the basketball team, to get a dream job, to find a soul mate, or to raise children. There is a tendency to have one's identity as synonymous with a chosen purpose. Traditionally, women tend to identify themselves with their relationships, while men identify themselves with their careers. When the children leave home or we retire, there may be a loss of the sense of self-identity—and a loss of life's meaning. When one can't work due to chronic illness or life tragedy, it can strip away a sense of identity. The associated stress can lead to mental or physical disease. Part of the healing process involves finding a new purpose that will realign the body, mind, and spirit. We need a purpose to which we are willing to give our lives. This is the power that gives us the energy to move forward in life.

Live life in love not out of obligation or in "should's." Live your life for *you*. Finding the true purpose of your life means reaching a state of alignment of your soul, mind, and body—and better health. Inner conflict obstructs your body's energy flow and causes disease. Follow your bliss.

Entrainment and the Power of Intention

The body consists of 100 trillion cells that perform different functions but work together for a greater cause: *you!* 100 trillion cells live, work, and die with the sole purpose of giving you life and consciousness. The greater the consciousness, the greater the energy to work toward a greater purpose.

An increase in consciousness brings about a corresponding increase in the overall energy level, leading to entrainment. Entrainment is an observable phenomenon in which there is a synchronization of a group into a common pattern, as set by a dominant object or individual because of energetic influence. The power of entrainment or influence is seen in inanimate objects like in a clock shop, when all the pendulum clocks start ticking at the same time. This phenomenon can be seen in humans, as well. Coeds who share a dorm or nuns in a convent have a synchronization of their menstrual periods. The collective memories of spouses or a loving couple are much greater than in each individual alone. Entrainment is an unseen energetic connection that one cell has with all the other cells of the body when aligned to a common goal. The same powerful energy unifies people who are working together toward the same mission. It is much easier to work out at the gym with other people who are also working out and have the same intention or purpose. By participating in a group intention, one carries the energy of not only oneself but the group, as well. There is a synergy that allows the group to accomplish what would not be able to be accomplished were each individual working separately.

One can see the power of entrainment in health. It has been proven that women who are struggling with cancer have a higher survival rate if they are involved in support groups. One sees the same phenomena with addictions and various support groups, such as Alcoholic's Anonymous (AA) or Narcotic's Anonymous (NA). Prior to the formation of Alcoholics Anonymous in the 1930s, having a diagnosis of alcoholism was essentially a death sentence that no one survived. The twelve-step program still remains a powerful tool for recovery. The program's power lies in the connection between participants having the same goal of abstinence and the spiritual belief of a power greater than themselves. There have been multiple scientific studies demonstrating that the sick have greater healing when they know they are loved and being prayed for. There is a power in seeking a purpose beyond self-interest and for the greater good of all, including oneself. The higher the goal's truth and love, the greater the power it has.

In the human experience, the connecting power of entrainment is through emotions. Our emotions are radiated in our aura. We all radiate consciousness as energy that interacts with others. A grieving person can walk into a room, and one can feel the energy of the group become depressed. Conversely, with an energetic and happy person, the room's energy gets elevated. Some have called the elevation "charisma" or "animal magnetism," which is an indescribable radiated energy. It has the ability to influence everything around it. The greater the alignment of purpose, the greater the influence. This purpose is intention.

Intention is setting the sail on the journey to accomplish your dream. Once a purpose from your spirit is set, intention coordinates and aligns your mind and body to achieve the goal. Once the mind is in alignment, new and coordinated neural connections and pathways in the brain direct all the cells of the body toward that intention. Your focus will allow you to perceive opportunities in the environment that would otherwise go unnoticed, helping you on the journey.

Transcendence of personal desires for a more noble cause gives one greater power to achieve that purpose. Professional athletes or performers oftentimes make gestures in gratitude, honor, or dedication to a higher being or a loved one. A transcendent purpose has a greater likelihood of higher accomplishment. In the 2012 Summer Olympics, I watched a member of the USA Olympic relay swim team swim beyond his normal ability to win a gold medal for the team while failing to achieve the same level of performance in an individual medley. Members of great sports teams working selflessly together perform at a higher level of success than as individual players. They can even compete successfully against a more talented team whose members don't work together. There are stories of soldiers who perform great acts of heroism and self-sacrifice. They are able to accomplish near-superhuman feats to save the lives of their companions, whether out of patriotism or for a greater cause.

Working with others toward a greater purpose helps us overcome personal fear and self-doubt. It is those fears and self-doubts that keep us from reaching our dreams. Transcending fear and self-doubt involves having the courage to surrender long-held erroneous beliefs. Fear or anger can sometimes give a short-term adrenaline rush and burst of energy, but they are non-sustainable and in the long run lead to fatigue and weakness. In contrast, being enveloped in one's purpose is energizing.

How does someone find purpose? A technique I've shared with my patients is writing their own eulogy. What would they like said about themselves at their funeral? What would they like to have accomplished before they die? Where would they spend more time? The process is something anyone can do, but it takes a great deal of soul searching. Take some time to reflect on it. Life's greatest rewards are not found in "things" accumulated, but rather in goals accomplished or relationships with others that were the most meaningful. What can you do starting today to live your purpose? What would make life worthwhile? What is your dream?

Define what that dream will do for you. It starts with the heart's desire and is energized and motivated by the heart. The mind imagines what obtaining the purpose would look like, sound like, and feel like. Can you imagine having accomplished your dream? Actually being there in the future and knowing how it feels? If you can't feel a pleasurable emotion with the obtaining of that dream, you won't have the energy to pursue it. Your purpose has to have enough emotional power that it is able to overcome any distraction, doubt, or obstacle.

Sometimes, there are pros and cons. The cons are the obstacles or resistance we create for ourselves. There may be self-doubt about being able to accomplish the goal. There may be resistance against what must be given up to achieve the goal. Doubt is not a bad thing but is something that has to be examined for its truth. Ask this of yourself: Do you want things to stay the way they are, or are you willing to do something about it? Obstacles and self-doubt will arise during all phases of the journey but can be used to create greater clarity, and overcoming the obstacles and self-doubt makes you stronger. This growth leads to greater wisdom. If the cons are transcended for a greater good, the obstacles disappear.

It is more about the journey than the destination. It is the *hero's journey*. What I have asked of my patients is to write their life's story to this moment. Write about all the tragedies and adversity until now. Then write about how they are going to overcome all their "demons" and obstacles of the future in order to get to their dream.

We discover things about ourselves that were hidden from our view—not only our weaknesses but also our strengths. Sometimes on the journey, we may discover that we are on the wrong path, but we realize we have the power to change course and open ourselves up to new, even greater possibilities. At the end of the journey, falsities are vanquished, and we realize that the true purpose of the journey was in becoming what we truly are. You realize that the resistance and obstacles you experienced were from the "lesser you" that you have transcended. The journey is about becoming a greater you, a more powerful you, a healthier you.

Putting Everything Together

Two of the most important studies of well-being are the Grant Study and Lewis Terman's "Genetic Study of Genius." Both studies are two of the longest-running longitudinal studies in history. The Grant Study followed 237 men for 68 years. The Terman Study started in 1921 and continues to the present, determining the factors that contribute to a long and happy life. What they have uncovered and are continuing to uncover are four main factors:

1. genetics,

2. a happy childhood,

3. positive and supportive relationships, and

4. gratitude and giving.

Our inheritance plays a major role in our health and well-being. Our heritage ranges from the place that we are born to our DNA molecules. Our inherited DNA not only determines the color of our hair and how tall we may become but also our susceptibility to certain illnesses and diseases. Some people are just more prone to living a longer life than others. As mentioned in the chapter on humor, stress has the effect of fraying and wearing down the bonds that hold our genes together and may make them more susceptible to cancer and other diseases.

We also have no choice in where we are born. Some countries have a higher average life expectancy than others. One environment could be very nurturing, while another could be a dangerous or stressful environment that can shorten life expectancy. When we are old enough, we can decide where we want to live and the amount of stress we want to put ourselves through.

It is known that major trauma and abuse in childhood lead to pain syndromes and health problems later in life. We have no choice about the family we are born into or events that occurred in our childhood. We do have a choice, however, in healing our trauma. The most powerful place to start is in forgiveness. Other techniques include being in gratitude for the lessons learned and how those events can make us more compassionate toward others who are suffering through the same events. Some people use humor to change perspectives and switch anger and shame into acceptance and joy.

The people we surround ourselves with play a major role in our health. Life is naturally attracted to the energy of love and repelled by fear and anger.

Love nurtures life. The more one learns to love, the more one is surrounded by love. Love is a nourishing energy to the cells of the body and creates better health. People who have loving spouses have greater longevity than people who are alone. Entrainment in love provides greater energy in sustaining life. The greater the loving relationships and interconnectedness, the greater the energy and power for healing.

Roseto, Pennsylvania, was a town of interest to epidemiologists and medical scientists (Stout, and Morrow). Rosetta had the lowest death rate following a heart attack than anywhere else in the country. Was it the type of diet, the water or air quality, the level of exercise, the lack of harmful habits (such as smoking), or some other risk factor that aided the heart attack survivors? What the researchers discovered was that the people of Rosetta had the same—or even worse—risk factors in comparison to the rest of the country. People who moved from this town to live in another part of the country would then develop a death rate similar to the national average. There was some protective quality provided by living in Rosetta.

What was the protective factor of Rosetta, Pennsylvania, that kept its inhabitance from dying from heart attacks? What was unique about the town was the great sense of community that was inclusive and protective. If your fence blew down in a windstorm, your neighbors would be there to help you build it back up again. If you were facing a major crisis in your life, people in the community would pull together to support you. The interconnectedness, compassion, and support of the community were the factors that provided health benefits for its members.

The last attribute both the Grant Study and Terman Study found regarding a long and happy life was somewhat surprising. One would think that the more material things one gets, the happier one would be. What creates a long and happy life, however, is not in getting or taking but is actually in the willingness to *give* to others.

I once asked myself, "What were the odds of me being born?" There were 1.5 billion people on the planet at the time of my conception. What were the chances of my parents finding each other and falling in love? What were the chances of that one sperm (out of 200–300 million sperm) fertilizing the egg? By my calculation, the chance of me being born, as it is with all of us, was one chance in 450 billion. That is some lottery! That is also the number of stars in a clear night sky. Even Jesus had a star. It was that star that led the three wise men to find him when he was born. Each one of us is as unique as a star and has our own special gifts. We have the choice about how bright we wish our star to shine. Our true sin is not to live our purpose, which is to discover and acknowledge our specialness and the gifts we were born with. At the end of our journey, when we uncover who we are in truth, we discover our gifts to be embraced and shared with the rest of the world. Sharing our gifts, when living our purpose, and applying our gifts in our work doesn't even feel like work. The giving is done out of the gratitude of being. The energy of giving of ourselves is returned to us in our well- being.

My Purpose

Caroline Myss is a medical intuitive, mystic, and author whose works I have studied. I wanted to meet her. A medical intuitive is able to assist in miraculous healings for conditions and diseases that are thought by traditional medicine to be incurable. She has the ability to look into a person's soul for the reason behind an illness. Once the person is made aware of the reason, he or she will often heal from the illness.

Caroline Myss worked with a neurosurgeon, C. Norm Shealy, to assist in healing his most difficult patients who had exhausted all other treatments traditional medicine had to offer. It was early in my journey that I became acquainted with Caroline Myss's work, and it reinforced my belief that the causes for diseases are more than physical. I felt that if I could be taught her technique, I would become a more effective healer and better able to discern if the root of an illness was coming from the body, the mind, or the spirit.

Caroline was giving a talk on self-esteem at a wellness conference in Jackson Hole, Wyoming, with other notable speakers such as Larry Dossey and Lama Dorjee. In the weeks preceding the conference, I asked myself, "If I have the chance, what is the one question I will ask her?" On the flight to the conference, after much contemplation, the answer arose: "What is God's purpose for me in this lifetime?"

A pre-speaker reception that included food and drinks was arranged for Caroline Myss, as well as the other speakers at the conference. When I entered the room, I looked over to where she was sitting, and there was a large group of people standing around her. I finally got up my nerve and started to walk up to her. As I reached her table, all the people surrounding her left at the same time, parting like the Red Sea.

"Ms. Myss?" I said.

"Oh, just call me Caroline," she replied in a warm greeting.

"Caroline, I just wanted to say, 'Thank you.' Your teachings have changed my life. I just have one question ..." Here, I chickened out. "Do you see people mistaking ego-based self-esteem with feeling secure?"

"Oh, all the time," she answered, somewhat exasperated. She began explaining the difference, but all I could think about was how I had blown my opportunity to ask my one question.

Suddenly, she stopped, turned to me, and said, "Oh, and by the way, I don't know what God's purpose is for you. But your heart is up here." She raised her hand several inches above her head. "And your head is down here," she said, gesturing with her other hand down at waist-level. "What you have to do is to release your attachments to get your head up to where your heart is."

Needless to say, I was dumbfounded. How was she able to answer my unspoken question? I spent the next several years following her advice, releasing my fears and my prejudices. Unless we learn to love ourselves, we can never heal. Healing and spiritual evolvement are the same. It has been my purpose to learn to transcend my feelings of unworthiness and undeservedness to uncover a state of self-love. I worked on overcoming self-righteousness and my fear of not living up to my potential.

I've continued to wonder what I'm supposed to do with my life. How can I be of greatest service and contribute to the world? What I've found is the more I undo my own judgments and prejudices, the more compassionate I am becoming toward my patients. I also find I am better able to realize the underlying root of a patient's disease. As one works to uncover the divinity in oneself, the purpose reveals itself. Ultimately, it is not about what one *does* but what one *becomes*.

Exercise

Write your own eulogy. What would you like said about you when you pass away? This allows you to do some introspection.

1. Write about all the things you have overcome in your life to get to this moment: all the resources and traits you have inside you that helped you survive and overcome all your obstacles. We all have

gifts or things we are good at doing—things that just by doing them, bring us pleasure.

2.   Write about the things you are grateful for in you life. Think about the things you may have taken for granted.

3.   Write about all the things that are really important to you now.

4.   Write your bucket list of things you would like to do before you die. Think about the things you have been putting off in your life. We never know when we are going to die.

5.   Think about what you can do for others in the future with your gifts that will make their lives better. Giving back to others not only helps them but also improves your life and life expectancy.

CHAPTER FOURTEEN

Paradox

"And he said unto them, Ye will surely say unto
me this proverb, Physician, heal thyself: whatever
we have heard done in Capernaum, do also here in
thy country."

—Luke 4:23 (KJV)

"I wanted to change the world, but I have found
that the only thing one can be sure of changing
is oneself."

—Aldous Huxley

"The world is round, and the place which may
seem like the end may also be the beginning."

—Ivy Baker Priest

P aradox by definition is a statement that seems contradictory, unbeliev-
able, or absurd but may actually be, in fact, true. A paradox is a statement that is self-contradictory in fact and hence, false. Paradox deals with
contradiction and the relationship of opposites. Opposites need each other to
establish meaning. When one takes a position, the opposite is automatically
created. One doesn't know hot unless one knows how cold; how light unless
one knows how dark; or how good unless one knows how bad. It is based,
however, on personal experience. A person from Texas may think the weather
is cold in Colorado, but a person from Alaska may think it is warm. Who is
right?

We tend to live in paradox for most of our lives when dealing with perceived opposites. Shakespeare's Hamlet said, "[F]or there is nothing either
good or bad, but thinking makes it so" (act 1, scene 2). We all want what we

perceive to be the good, but what is good? If all we experienced was good, would we really appreciate it? When things are good, we get comfortable, lazy, and complacent. Only when things are bad do we look for an escape, a new solution, and become creative.

Paradox can exist in concepts such as hope and love. Hope can be man's greatest asset for survival and provides meaning and purpose in one's life (dreams). When unfulfilled, hope can lead to broken dreams, heartache, and unrequited love. We all want to find our soul mate: the one person who completes us and makes us happy. The hope of a soul mate, however, may exist as romantic love, in which the other person is expected to meet all of one's needs and desires. The belief that something outside yourself can make you feel love or find happiness is erroneous. We may subconsciously look for someone who compensates for our deficiencies or has characteristics that we wish we had for ourselves. A victim will attract a rescuer. An abuser will attract someone willing to be abused. Understanding paradox, to attract the person with certain characteristics we want in our lives, we have to become that person and develop those characteristics in ourselves. Like tends to attract like.

Relationships are ultimately about personal growth. Our soul mate might be our worst enemy, put in our lives to teach us about ourselves, our blind spots, or our shortcomings. Who teaches us more about ourselves and our judgments than our enemies? Instead of blaming another person for something we think they did wrong, we need to try and understand that their life experience may be completely different from our own and that what we consider wrong may be totally acceptable in another culture. If you get upset in the relationship, there is something you need to discover about yourself—something keeping you from your higher self that needs to be let go.

It is human nature to want to believe someone else is truthful when he or she believes the same as we do. It is the foundation of trust. We tend to trust others who are like us, and we tend to distrust anyone who is not like us. We also tend to believe people who tell us what we want to hear, even when what they tell us is not true. Compassion comes from the understanding of differences. It has been said that you don't know another person until you walk in his shoes. To overcome paradox, we must take responsibility for our choices and how we look at others. To transcend paradox is to understand that true courage and power come from surrendering judgment.

In his book, *The Dancing Wu Li Masters,* Gary Zukav wrote, "True understanding involves breaking the barrier of paradox." Understanding involves surrendering emotional attachments or judgment. We are able to gain a broader and greater perspective when we accept that our personal experience, opinions and beliefs are limited and illusory. Only through understanding and transcending paradox can we unlock the mystery of life and of existence.

Healing and Paradox

The paradox of becoming a powerful healer is to become the patient. In other words, when a healer steps into a patient's sense of reality, the healer may then gain insight into the cause of presenting symptoms and has a better chance of influencing healing. Such understanding helps establish a greater rapport and trust. It can also expose the underlying root that may be causing the presenting symptoms. A healer who overcomes a disease is best able to help guide others who suffer from the same disease.

A powerful Hawaiian healing process is called *Ho'oponopono.* Dr. Ihaleakala Hew Len worked in healing the criminally insane at Hawaii State Hospital. Instead of directly working on the patients, he said, "I was simply healing the part of me that created them." In other words, the world you perceive is your creation. What you perceive and experience is a projection of what is inside of you. The problem is not with them, but the perceptions that are inside you. You must change yourself to change "them." You must change your consciousness to change the world, and it all begins and ends with love. It all comes full circle, and that is the paradox.

A patient's consciousness and beliefs plays a large role in the susceptibility to disease and the success of treatment. Additionally, the healer's level of consciousness also influences the success of healing. The higher consciousness of unconditional love and truth overcome conditions that are incurable with psychology, medication, or surgery, and can also make conventional treatment even more effective.

Love heals. What people seek is love. People don't say, "God *has* love"; they say, "God *is* love." The law of attraction dictates that you attract what you are. Love is attractive. When you radiate an energy of love, you attract love to you. How does one find love? One doesn't acquire love but uncovers it from within. One finds love by becoming and radiating love to others. People want love but are afraid of love because of the fear of being hurt or rejected. Learning to love takes courage. *A Course in Miracles* teaches that God is love and that the opposite of love is fear. To find love, one must let go of fear.

In the book, *The Art of Happiness*, Dalai Lama said, "What we all seek is happiness. Happiness comes from four things: health, wealth, worldly satisfaction (our relationships with our partner, family, community, and the world), and enlightenment (Spirituality)." The search for enlightenment is the pursuit of ultimate truth. The strategy to obtain each component of happiness is the same process. The factors that are keeping you from wealth are the same factors that are keeping you from good health, which, in turn, are the same factors affecting your relationships. It takes a change in beliefs and subsequently, a change in oneself that provides the opening to allow receiving all aspects of happiness. The ego mind believes the way to win is by resisting and fighting for what is wanted. We are led to believe that achieving these things comes from outside ourselves. The truth is that happiness comes from inside, out—not outside, in. We have the innate ability to heal, create wealth, and have better relationships, but it comes from changing ourselves. We cannot be a victim and must take personal responsibility to facilitate the change. By removing our judgments and finding humor, we are better able to understand and have a better connection with others. By living life in gratitude and awareness, we realize how much we do have. This eliminates the obstacles of fear that hinders our prosperity. Improved health comes from forgiving ourselves and others. Ultimately, happiness comes from surrendering the old self for a new and improved self. Letting go brings you what you want.

The paradox of eliminating pain or losing weight is to learn to surrender to the pain or the hunger. By resisting it or acting on it, the pain or the hunger get stronger and stay longer. As we discussed in a previous chapter, we strengthen the thought and feeling by thinking, "Stop!" or, "Resist!" We can realize that pain and hunger are just sensations that will dissipate with time. Also, by naming the sensation (e.g., by calling it "hunger" or "pain"), we strengthen its power over us. We bring up past memories of the same feeling and often, images of the worst-case scenario. We may visualize the Donner Party or even death, pressing us to satisfy the feeling with action. As with Pavlov's dog, if you eat when feeling the sensation of "hunger" or take a pill when feeling "pain," you positively reinforce and strengthen the sensation. To extinguish the feeling, surrender to the feeling with neutrality, acceptance, and non-action. To more rapidly extinguish it, we can tell ourselves we want more of the sensation. In paradox, resisting something makes it stronger and brings it closer. Desiring something moves it further from you.

The spirit is more powerful than the mind, and the mind is more powerful than the body. Enlightenment leads to a higher level of consciousness and being. Higher consciousness leads to a greater sense of well-being, wealth, and oneness with others. As one lives in more truth, one has more power to transcend illnesses that have roots in lower conscious states. A higher level of consciousness allows one to better empathize with others and form closer, richer relationships.

Throughout this book we have presented various aspects of healing. The driving forces to healing are devotion and courage. Overcoming old belief patterns and fears takes courage. The devotion to purpose—to get back up after failing or feeling defeated—takes commitment. In a paradox, therefore, failures are more important than wins in developing inner strength and fortitude. It is more about the journey than the destination and what one becomes along the way.

Spiritual openings oftentimes arise through the depths of catastrophe and despair. At times of catastrophe, it becomes apparent that old paradigms and belief patterns no longer work. "Hitting bottom" has the potential to create spiritual growth. The Taoists would say within every crisis lies opportunity. It allows for creativity. New solutions arise out of the destruction of old beliefs that no longer work. Oftentimes, when faced with a serious health crisis, one will be open to seek esoteric remedies that wouldn't normally be considered.

The key to higher consciousness that allows for greater happiness and health is to uncover the divinity within. Ramana Maharshi, a modern-day mystic, once said that a higher level of consciousness can be achieved by one of two paths: by discovering who one is or by surrendering all one thinks one is. In the end, they are the same path. Joseph Luft and Harry Ingham created the Johari window as a means of self-discovery (Figure 3).

The window consists of four panes of glass and represents the window into one's soul. One pane of glass is completely transparent, two panes are 50% opaque, and the fourth pane is completely dark. The completely clear pane ("open") is what you see in yourself and let others see in you. One of the 50% opaque panes ("hidden") is what you see in yourself but won't let others see in you because of guilt and shame. The other 50% pane ("blind") is what you don't see in yourself because of denial but what others *do* see in you. The final, completely dark pane ("unknown") is what you don't see in yourself and what other people don't see in you—because you've never done it. You have never explored that aspect of yourself out of fear, ignorance, or judgment.

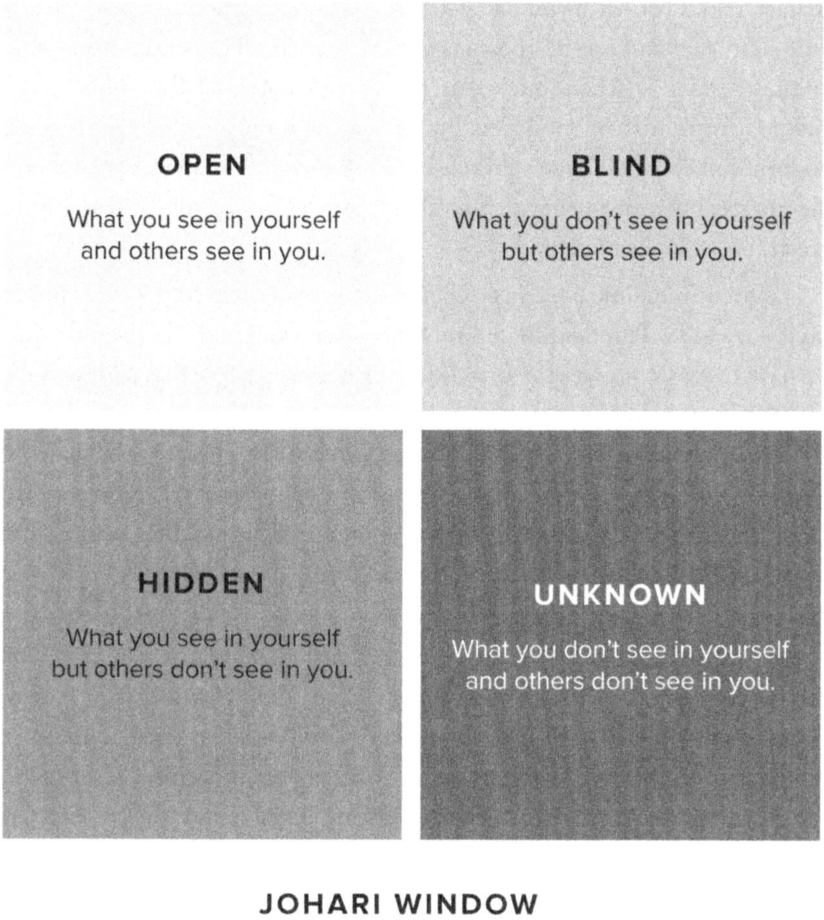

OPEN

What you see in yourself and others see in you.

BLIND

What you don't see in yourself but others see in you.

HIDDEN

What you see in yourself but others don't see in you.

UNKNOWN

What you don't see in yourself and others don't see in you.

JOHARI WINDOW

Figure 3: Johari Window

Denial is based on fear, which you compensate with pride. As previously discussed, denial is a defense mechanism to keep the truth about yourself from your conscious self. Such a view does not allow us to see our frailties; it also prevents us from seeing ourselves with inner honesty. Maintaining old beliefs affects our health and our relationships. Only through the power of humility can we unravel these untruths and heal.

Deepak Chopra once said that the characteristics that you dislike in others are characteristics you have in yourself that you deny or won't acknowledge. In psychology, it is called "projection": a defense mechanism of the ego. Chopra also said that the characteristics that you admire in others are characteristics you wish you had yourself. I believe all the admirable qualities reside in the darkest unknown part of oneself. The dark, mysterious, unknown pane is where one's true power and potential live. This pane is guarded from our consciousness by fear and ignorance, which lead to self-doubt. An iceberg illustrates this concept. One-eighth of an iceberg is seen at the surface, but a vast majority is hidden from view in the subconscious of the ocean (i.e., 88% is hidden).

Oftentimes, one needs a teacher of integrity to help find what is hidden from one's view. President Franklin Delano Roosevelt said, "[T]he only thing we have to fear is fear itself." It is the Zen Buddhists belief that all fear is illusion. Walk straight ahead no matter what. People tend to fear the unknown, but the unknown is where power resides. One of the greatest fears is that of death or nonexistence. You are not who you think you are, however. True power comes from reprogramming the brain's software beliefs to become a more powerful being. As Eckart Tolle would say, "[You must] lose yourself to find yourself."

I realized that disease may be a symptom of something else in the hidden or unknown. I needed to remove my own preconceptions and increase my awareness to discover it. I use the metaphor of our bodies as cars. I'm in my car (body), and if *my* windshield is dirty and my *patient's* windshield is dirty, then I can't see who or what is driving their car. I am unable to see my patient's soul and motivation. Only by cleaning my own windshield—my window—do I have greater clarity and any chance to see them for who they are. This leads to greater rapport and greater healing.

When we clean off our windows, through integrity and forgiveness of ourselves and others, and explore our fears and judgments, then we become transparent to the world and to ourselves. We forgive ourselves for the things we try to keep hidden from others. Through the compassion of stepping into another person's shoes, we realize patterns of behavior that may have sabotaged relationships in the past. When we explore the unknown part of ourselves with courage and humility, we become what we dream of becoming. We eliminate all doubt and develop a knowing of the self and of the world. We allow the divine light of what we are to shine out and illuminate the path for others on their journey.

Grey Wolf

Throughout my time of practicing medicine, I never knew what I would find when I opened the door to the waiting room to call in a patient. I have met some unique individuals. I had one patient who thought he was a vampire. Another patient was completely physically healthy but gave herself a disabling diagnosis and rode around the community in an electric wheelchair. Once, there was a Native American woman (I'll call "Mary") who stood in the center of the waiting room when I called her in. She was a short woman in her mid-fifties with few teeth and straight, disheveled, jet-black hair rising out from her scalp like a troll doll. She wore an old wrap and carried a tall staff of gnarled wood. She looked like a witch. She had multiple medical problems, including diabetes and heart, lung, and kidney disease. She had severe neuropathy and failing eyesight. We talked about her ailments, and I realized there was nothing I could do for her medically. We talked about her life, and it became clear that more than her physical ailments, her suffering came from her spirit. I asked her why she didn't seek healing from her elders or medicine man. She said all her elders were dead, and she had nowhere else to go. Despite having adequate health care closer to home, she religiously travelled over a hundred miles every month to see me. I really didn't see what I was doing for her, but she slowly smiled and said, "You have good energy."

For some reason, I have been drawn to Native American culture and wanted to learn more of their healing techniques. After Tom Ballestieri's talk in Santa Fe, I went up and asked him if he knew of a shaman or Native American healer I could consult about the woman. He gave me the name and phone number of Grey Wolf.

Grey Wolf was an Inuit shaman living in Southern California at the time. Grey Wolf told me that when he was a child, like other Native American children, he had to leave his tribe, get his hair cut short, and was forbidden to speak his native language. He got involved in the Catholic Church and eventually became a Catholic deacon when he was sixteen years old. He traveled all over the world with "Father John," performing exorcisms.

When I first talked to Grey Wolf on the phone, he asked me what my ancestry was. I told him my grandparents came from Japan. He told me that he had been to Japan on numerous occasions and had studied with shamans and healers in Australia, New Zealand, Africa, and North, Central, and South America. He said the Eskimo man's face on the tail of Alaskan Airline jets was his father.

Grey Wolf had been given the opportunity to travel and study healing from indigenous healers all over the world. Once, he laughed and said he thought he had known a lot about telepathy—until he spent time with the Aborigines in Australia and realized he knew nothing compared to those people. He taught me about Native American philosophy and about using energy and how it was used in healing. He talked about healing from "soul retrieval."

When I arrived back in Chico, I arranged a telephone call between Mary and Grey Wolf. I left the room of my office, and they talked for an hour. When she emerged, she was in a beatific state and seemed to finally have a look of peace on her face that I had never seen in her before. She thanked me and told me that I was going to be a great healer. I never saw her again.

I studied with Grey Wolf and his female partner, Paah Pooh for almost two years. There were many amazing adventures. At the end, Paah Pooh called me at home and said that she and Grey Wolf had talked about me. She said I had learned as much as I needed to know. She said that I had to take that knowledge and "become it."

I had dedicated the last ten years to studying different aspects of healing from both the mind and spiritual perspectives. Exploring different psychological and spiritual practices to find ways to help others heal helped me heal, as well. I found I could no longer practice medicine the way I had my whole career. Sometimes, there is an inner knowing of changes we need to make in our lives. We keep ourselves living our same lives out of fear and denial. I decided to leave my career: the money, the prestige, and the big house. I had to respect the feeling of something else that I knew in my heart I needed to do. I walked away from my old life and spent a week with a Yaqui shaman before doing a vision quest. Alone, I fasted and walked the desert for three days. I opened up all my closet doors and let my skeletons and demons out: all the things I was ashamed of and felt guilty for, fearful of, and angry about. I took responsibility for all that had happened to me. It was a truly humbling experience.

I came back home exhausted and didn't want to see anyone. I barely had enough energy to go to the grocery store to buy food. I would develop muscle cramps at night and grind my teeth from the pain. Eventually, with the support and love of family and friends, I slowly made it back into the world. My father died two months later, and before his death, I was able to spend quality time with him and make peace with him. My mother became ill after his death. I sold my home and moved in with her. She had four major surgeries over the next year and a half. I helped take care of her, made peace, and developed a much closer relationship with her—and myself.

I visited with the Yaqui shaman several months later and told him of my experiences since I had left after studying with him. He said, "Kelley, you've come full circle. You've given up everything you thought you were. You've made peace with your father before his death. You made peace with your mother and are taking care of her. You came back home. You moved back into the womb, waiting for your rebirth."

It reminds me of the parable that Joseph Campbell spoke of from Friedrich Nietzsche's *Thus Spake Zarathustra*. We all start our lives as camels that have baggage (burdens) placed on our backs. The heavier the burden, the stronger the camel becomes. It is the purpose of the camel to walk into the desert. Once the camel enters the desert, it becomes the lion, and it is the purpose of the lion to slay its dragon. The dragon has green scales all over its body, and on each scale it says, "Thou shall ... Thou shall ...": all the "shoulds" we place on ourselves in a life of obligation. Once the lion slays the dragon, it becomes a child.

It became obvious to me that to become a better healer, I would have to strip away the ego. It is the ego that separates and prevents us from truly connecting with one another. Like Jesus said in the book of Luke, "Physician, heal thyself." The more I work on my own prejudices and attachments, the better healer I become.

The journey has come full circle: from the dream I had in self-confrontation to the realization of the truth. I am responsible for my reality and my happiness, and I have the power to change it. I have come to the understanding that there is no cause and effect; there is just *being*. In becoming, we create our own miracles. The paradox is that achieving a state of being is through surrender and acceptance of self and others in love. This love is God. May you all be blessed on your path.

"The Serenity Prayer" by Reinhold Niebuhr (1892–1971)

God, give us the grace to accept with serenity the things that cannot be changed,

Courage to change the things which should be changed,
and the Wisdom to distinguish the one from the other.
Living one day at a time,
Enjoying one moment at a time,
Accepting hardship as a path to peace,
Taking, as Jesus did, this sinful world as it is,
Not as I would have it,
Trusting that You will make all things right,
If I surrender to Your will,
So that I may be reasonably happy in this life,

And supremely happy with You forever in the next. Amen.

Epilogue

After I left my job of twenty-one years and my mother had fully recovered from her illnesses and surgeries, I continued my studies and started to write this book. At some point, I hoped to have the opportunity to see what impact my awakening would have on patients. I was given the opportunity to work at an Adventist Health clinic in Paradise, California. How many people can say they work in Paradise? I started the integrative pain management program: a more holistic approach to patient care. I started to build the program from scratch, and it consisted of four components. I would do the initial evaluation, order the appropriate tests and medications, and direct the patient's care. The program also included behavioral health for counseling and biofeedback; life-change medicine for diet, nutrition, and sleep; traditional physical therapy; and occupational therapy for Feldenkrais therapy. The program dealt directly with pain but more importantly, addressed and treated other aspects of a patient's suffering (i.e., social isolation, estrangement from family, guilt, fear, anger, and low self-esteem). I wanted to see if merging the traditional medical approach with a spiritual one would have a greater impact in healing. Being a spiritually based health system, they were more receptive and supportive of my project than a non-faith-based organization might be. Addressing spiritual healing is part of the Adventist Health's mission statement and vision.

As previously mentioned, the Dalai Lama has said that what we all seek in life is happiness. Happiness comes from four things: health, wealth, worldly satisfaction (our relationships with our partner, family, community, and the world), and enlightenment. I feel the same limiting or false beliefs that affect people's health also affect their wealth and relationships. It is my hope that raising an individual's level of consciousness will improve not only their pain and illness but also relationships and finances.

Lifestyle Medicine's CREATIONS Health Assessment form was filled out by the patient on their initial visit and every few months thereafter, to see if we were making progress in different aspects of the patient's life. CREATIONS is an acronym for Choices, Rest, Environment, Activity, Trust, and Soreness. We would grade the patient's responses and were able to monitor any improvement we were able to make in each area with participation in the program. The clinic provided me with a graduate student from Chico State University to assist in data collection and statistical analysis.

The patient population was primarily the disadvantaged. Poverty tends to breed poverty through the indigent's beliefs and actions. It was my belief that if the program would work with this patient population, it would work with anyone. Personality Assessment Inventory (PAI) was performed on each participant to get an idea of personality characteristics. The traits that were common among all the patients were lack of trust, external locus of control, and low self-esteem. Often during the initial interview, I would hear horrendous stories of childhood abuse, parental neglect, substance abuse, and dysfunctional, self-destructive behavior. Trust is established during the earliest years of childhood in maternal-child bonding. Locus of control is either internal or external. The patients I treated felt they had no control over their lives and that their environment or other people dictated their lives. They developed "learned helplessness" and an apathy about life. Low self-esteem came from lack of self-worth and deservedness after years of childhood and early adulthood criticism. The patients were also socially isolated because of a lack of social support.

The program addressed the mind and body components of healing. The one component of the program that was missing was the spiritual. I wanted to emphasize the areas of deficiencies discovered in the PAI. To address the social isolation, I started a pain support group. There is great power in groups to develop camaraderie and maintain motivation. I elicited the assistance of the hospital chaplain, Brad Brown, and a marriage-and-family counselor, Barry Pratt, to teach each of the principles presented in this book every other week. Stephanie McDonald and later Berlanta Decroix and Amanda Mulrennen were the coordinators, facilitators, and cheerleaders for the patients and the program. Upon completion of the course, we held a graduation to which patients could invite friends and family. Public speaking is one of the scariest things for many people, and getting up in front of an audience takes tremendous courage. It is also life-changing. At the ceremony and celebration, the participants would get up and tell their "hero's journey": what they had learned and how they planned to change their lives.

For many of the participants, the whole experience was transformative. One patient's adult children came up to me after the graduation, shook my hand, and thanked me for "giving us our mom back." I recently had a patient tell me that if he hadn't participated in the support group, he would not be here (he had been suicidal). It completely changed his life. Graduates expressed better relationships, some had lost weight, and others had started working again. Most said they still had pain but that it was no longer disabling and the focus of their lives.

They all thanked me, but I knew it wasn't me. I can't heal anyone. The patients did the hard work and stayed committed. I just guided them and was so grateful to be able to observe their transformation. The patient's faith and devotion had healed them. There is an old adage: "Give a man a fish, and you feed him for a day. Teach a man to fish, and you feed him for a lifetime." For me, true healing is about empowering and teaching patients to heal themselves.

There is the story of the "hundredth monkey." In 1952, off the coast of Japan, there was an island of monkeys that were being studied by a team of scientists. Sweet potatoes were left by the scientists in the dirt and sand for the monkeys to eat. The monkeys enjoyed the taste of the sweet potatoes but found that the sand and grit made the potatoes unpalatable. One day, a young monkey named Imo discovered that by washing the potato in the salty ocean, much of the sand could be removed. She taught the technique to her mother and playmates, and they taught other monkeys. More of the monkeys had learned to clean the sweet potatoes until ninety-nine monkeys had learned the technique. By the hundredth monkey, something magical happened. Suddenly, all the monkeys on the island washed their potatoes without being taught. That is not the end of the story, however. The scientists discovered that monkey colonies on other surrounding islands began washing their sweet potatoes, as well—without being taught.

People evolve with inspiration or desperation. Humanity is in a state of transition (shift). Change is a part of life. Beliefs and values that have been maintained by society with no integrity cannot survive. We already see unrest among the people; Something is not quite right. Indigenous Americans have been aware of the shift for quite some time. The Hopi have said that the beginning of the transition will be signaled by the "mark (scratch) of the bear claw." The scratch is translated as the bar code used in commerce by the financial system. It will be the first to collapse. There will be those who will be in denial and adhere to the old values, trying to maintain the flawed status quo. Others will be lost in panic, anger, desperation, and hopelessness. There will be others, however, who will evolve and create something new. Charles Darwin said it was not the strongest, fastest, most prolific, or longest-lived that survives, but the most adaptable and flexible. Through crisis comes creation and evolution.

My teacher David Hawkins lived in Sedona, Arizona. During my free time on my trips there, I would enjoy going through the many art galleries. When I went in 2009, however, more than half of the art galleries had closed. I went into one of the remaining art galleries and talked to the curator, who was a young woman. I told her how sad I was to see so many of the art galleries out of business. She said the 2008 financial collapse not only affected the businesses but many of her friends, as well. They thought they were going to make a fortune by stretching their finances and buying multiple houses they thought would continue to appreciate in value. When the financial crash happened, it led to the loss of jobs, bankruptcy, and divorce. An interesting thing happened, however. The friends pulled together and helped each other. If someone was out of work, he or she would babysit the other friend's children. Another would do the housecleaning. Another would do the home maintenance. Still another would do the shopping or cooking. A supportive community formed in which each member had a responsibility for developing a role in giving to the community. It was finding one's personal gift to share with others that would, in turn, sustain themselves.

The shift allows each of us to evolve in our level of consciousness. It will allow each of us to surrender who we were to become part of the solution. It will allow us to create a world worth inheriting for future generations by becoming what we were meant to be. It is the evolution to a new being, which Dr. Hawkins calls "Homo Spiritus."

Conscious awareness is shared by all of humanity. By raising one's own level of consciousness, you help raise the consciousness of all humankind. As an individual, you can't single-handedly effect change in human suffering in the Middle East or Africa. By changing yourself, however, you help to change the world. By being responsible and becoming a role model for others, you can help others to evolve. Like the transformation of the hundredth monkey, all humanity can change to a higher level of being when a critical mass is reached. Laser lights are known not to deviate from a straight line. If a laser is sent into the infinite universe, however, then the gravitational pull from stars and other galactic forces curves the light and, I believe, eventually brings it back to its source. The light of God that you send out eventually returns to you. Forgiveness for others leads to forgiveness of oneself. Radiating gratitude for others leads to an inner sense of gratitude for life. Many religions think of God as transcendent, but the light of God is also immanent (inside of you). It just has to be uncovered. The most direct route to discovering God's divinity can be through the discovery of divinity within. Similarly, by realizing one's interconnectedness to all things, one finds oneself.

How the Brain Works

The Nervous System

The human nervous system structurally consists of the brain, spinal cord, and peripheral nerves (Figure 4). Outside of the brain and spinal cord, there are three different types of nerves based on function: the sensory, motor, and autonomic nervous systems. The **sensory** nerves bring information up to the brain, and the brain makes the decision on the best course of action. **Motor** nerves send signals back down to the body, telling the body what to do and how to act.

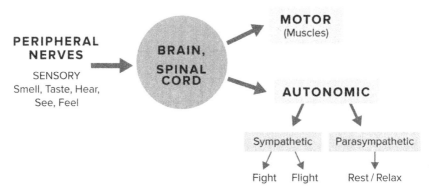

Figure 4: The Human Nervous System

The Autonomic Nervous System

The autonomic nerves regulate and synchronize the body's organs through electrical (nerve) and chemical (hormones) signals. The automatic nervous system regulates the body's temperature, heart rate, blood pressure, digestion, etc. It becomes activated when something in the body or environment is perceived as desired or as a threat. The automatic nervous system has two different systems: the **sympathetic** and the **parasympathetic**. If the stimulus is perceived as being something that is desired, the parasympathetic system becomes active. Things desired lead the parasympathetic system to decrease the heart rate and blood pressure, increase the digestive system, and provide a sense of calm. The sympathetic system becomes activated when the body perceives a threat, provoking the body's fight-or-flight response. The sympathetic system speeds up the heart rate, pumping more blood, energy, and oxygen to the muscles when strength is needed and dilating the pupils of the eyes to increase alertness and vigilance. Once the perceived threat has passed, the parasympathetic system works to slow the body down to rest.

The Brain

There are five different types of senses the brain receives from specialized sensory nerve cells that allow the brain to see, hear, taste, smell, and feel information both in the body and in the environment. The brain is the control center and directs the body to perform the most appropriate action or behavior based on what information it receives from the sensory system about the environment—and what's going on in the body.

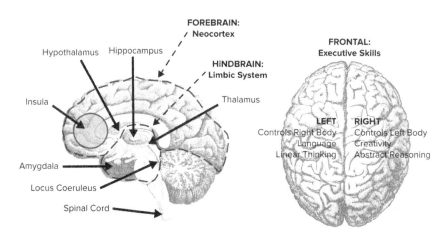

Figure 5: The Brain

There are two basic parts of the brain: the hindbrain and the forebrain. The **hindbrain** is the primitive brain. It lies deep in the brain structure and is made up of two parts. One part of the hindbrain receives sensory information inside the body (i.e., thirsty, hungry, too hot, too cold, in pain, etc.). The second part of the hindbrain receives information from the environment outside of the body (i.e., danger, food, pleasure, etc.). The **forebrain** is also called neocortex (*neo* means "new") and encases the hindbrain like a large bike helmet, forming the surface of the brain. It also consists of three parts: the left and right cerebral hemispheres and the frontal lobe. The left side controls the right side of the body and is also involved in language, memory, and concrete, linear reasoning. The right side controls the left side of the body and is involved in abstract reasoning (thinking "outside the box") and creativity. In other words, the left is the intellect, and the right is the inventor and artist. The frontal lobe is the brain's governor and is able to transcend existing consciousness to higher levels, overriding primitive instincts in developing compassion for others.

The hindbrain is the most ancient and primitive part of the brain and is at the core of the brain. Some call it the "reptile brain." Psychologists call it the **ego**, and science calls it the **limbic system**. Its function could be called the heart of animal nature, providing emotion to experience and directing the experience to be stored into memory.

The ego mind operates on an animal-instinct level, as previously mentioned, and is related to survival: to pursue that which is desired or to avoid that which is perceived as dangerous. Ego was born with the dawn of life itself. It is in all living animals. It is totally based on self-interest, with no regard for the welfare of others. The ego brain is the first to be developed and operational at birth. It is only later—with age, experience, and teaching from parents—that the outer neocortex of the brain develops. This is where all the memories and experiences are stored and retrieved in learning to allow a more efficient and rapid response.

The sensory pathways enter the brain through the **thalamus**. The thalamus acts as the brain's central railway station. The brain receives a constant flow of sensory signals. If there is something perceived to be out of the ordinary, the signal gets sent to the limbic system, which consists of the locus ceruleus, amygdala, hippocampus, and hypothalamus. The **locus ceruleus** brings the perception to conscious awareness. From there, it is sent to the **amygdala**, where value and emotion are attached to the perception. If there is a perceived threat, the signal gets sent to the **hypothalamus** and **HPA** (hypothalamic/pituitary/adrenal axis), which lead to what is known as the fight-or-flight response by activating the autonomic nervous system and stimulating

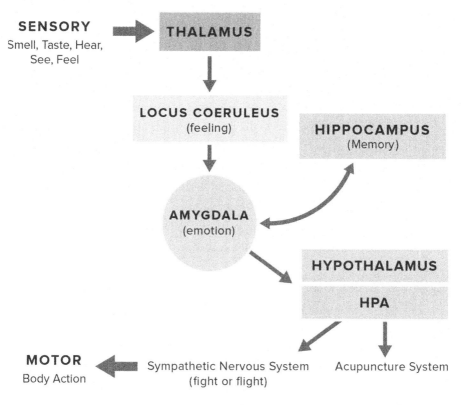

Figure 6: Limbic System

the release of hormones such as cortisol and adrenalin. The sensory signal also gets sent to the **hippocampus**, which converts the perception into meaning and memory and stores it in various parts of the neocortex. If the same or similar sensory perception is re-experienced, the memory is retrieved, and the body can respond quickly—even without conscious awareness (i.e., the **subconscious**). Therefore, memories are the subconscious. More than 95% of body functions are run by the subconscious.

There is a difference between feeling and emotion. Feeling involves the sensation or perceptions the body experiences in the present (e.g., the temperature, firmness of the seat, sound volume, etc.). Emotions are the value that is placed on the experience (e.g., fear, desire, anger, etc.). Therefore, feelings deal with perception *now*, and emotions are based on *prior* similar perceptions and the judgment of those sensations.

Brain Plasticity

It has also been observed that different areas of the brain can change their functions to compensate for damaged or removed portions of brain. In childhood blindness or deafness, the area of the brain normally dedicated to those functions then evolves to performing and augmenting other cerebral functions. The structure of the brain was thought for many years by scientists to be static and rigid. Injuries and impairments to the brain were felt to be permanent. More recent research has shown the brain to be more flexible and adaptable than originally thought. After adolescence, the number of brain cells progressively declines. The brain is capable of continued new memories and learning. Brain cells are different from the other cells of the body that continually replace themselves. The total number of neurons in the brain may not increase in later life, but the number of connections between neurons, called **synapses**, can be unlimited.

There are examples of the brain's capacity for flexibility occurring in humans. The natural animal tendency is for self-preservation. Women who become new mothers, however, commonly sacrifice their own needs and even compromise their own survival for the benefit of their young. For men, an override for personal survival most commonly occurs during war. There is a rewiring of brain patterns and pathways through the right prefrontal cortex and **insula** to the egoic limbic system, leading to more compassionate behavior. The insula links emotions to the body's regulation. The right brain's insula is involved with awareness of internal conditions and regulates blood pressure and pain perception. The insula is also the place of empathy. When observing suffering in another, one imagines one's own suffering.

The brain is the control center for the rest of the body and directs the body toward a given action. It is now realized that the brain is more dynamic and flexible than previously imagined. An understanding of the full potential of the brain is just now being studied with new excitement and possibilities. We are capable of new learning and behavioral changes, both of which can have an impact on changing our brain pathways and chemistry, leading to beneficial effects on our body's health and our relationships.

Testimonials

There is a difference between people who learn about change and those who follow through and do the work. I have had the privilege of watching the transformation of people who had the courage and dedication to change their lives. Here are their testimonies to the process.

"I'm more aware of how my pain effects me inwardly and outwardly. I am able now to take time to heal spiritually and physically. Now I have the tools to be successful in putting my chronic pain aside and perhaps going on to do things I've thought impossible due to the pain. I can use all the tools. I can feel better." —Stacy

"[The program] made me aware that there were others going through much of the same trials and tribulations as I." —David

"The program has helped with tools that I can use so that I may cope even better. So far, I have a new outlook. I am thinking about things in the future instead of the past. I am making plans to do things that I haven't thought of in years—productive things. Things that others might like. Not thinking about pain all the time is really great. I would encourage anyone who has problems with pain to try the program." —Brent

"I have been grateful to have received new (tools)—ways to deal with my problems, mentally as well as physically. I feel a lot healthier and have a better outlook on life." —Marlene

"The lessons Dr. Otani and Barry provided have had a huge impact on my life. I lost nearly sixty pounds. [They] helped with anger and even disciplining my children. There is not enough paper to tell you how this program has changed and enriched my life. Group has helped me identify with other people and also taught me to let go of things I was hanging onto that were causing me other kinds of pain." —Trisha

"It has given me people to trust in and has helped me in relieving some pain. The fact that spirituality is honored, utilized, and encouraged is a blessing. This is an *incredible* program. This is an incredible group to work with." —Rosemary

"Oh my! It has affected my life in so many ways! It has opened my eyes to what my life could be." —Theresa

"Dr. Otani has given me *all* the tools necessary for forgiveness of self and others. Each forgiveness for me came with feel-good tears and a much lighter feeling inside, especially [in] my head. Now, when thoughts appear of my past with others, they are fond thoughts with warm feelings, and then I smile. It takes time to change negative thoughts into positive [ones]. It is worth it in order to set yourself *free*. Thank you all so very much." —Nina

"It has allowed me to not feel alone in my pain. I did not know that this kind of program existed, and I hope this kind of thing grows to help others in pain." —Dorothy

"Group was very helpful to me because I did not know I needed some form of therapy. I have never been to therapy, so I did not see the advantages. Now I do." —Glenna

"The group with Dr. Otani was especially helpful to me. The exercises helped me to process my negative hurtful life experiences in a way I had not been able to. That has helped me to begin the healing. I am *so* grateful! This is life-altering!" —Tana

"[It] helped change my attitude toward life and others. I believe that the pain has grown less through divine help. It helped me be more relaxed around people." —James

"It has 'saved' me twice: [first] with my initial pain and emotional problems, then again when I was re-injured and turned to this same group for support once again." —Phyllis

"The ability to get my mind off of the daily pain is awesome. The tools are helping me in other parts of my life also." —Rene

"I'm more accepting of the pain I have, and my pain level is lower." —Ruth

"I learned through forgiveness, meditation ,and being grateful that those things helped to alleviate a lot of my pain both emotionally and physically." —Anonymous

"Very helpful for throughout-the-day control. I can make it further until nighttime and relaxation time." —James

"So far, a better bit of insight as to how I can release some of the stress and make it easier to find more comfort ... in pain relief." —Pat

"I feel that the tools I gained through the group are necessary to help me work [through] the difficult roadblocks that I have placed in my own recovery." —Robin

"The support group was amazing! I really learned a lot about how the mind and body and spirit work together as one. It really put together all the pieces. Oh my goodness, where to start? The combination of all the different stuff has been a real life-saver for me. At first I was skeptical when he said he had a plan for me, but I was willing to try anything. It took awhile for me to truly surrender and embrace all the programs and put them together. I did, and all I can say is WOW!! I know I still have a lot to learn, and I'm excited to see where this amazing journey is going to take me. I can't thank everyone enough for not giving up on me when I had given up on myself [and] for bringing me out of the darkness and into the light. This program is truly amazing. Thank you so very much." —Kim

"Just being involved with all my other classmates [who] are going through the same thing I'm going through and knowing that I'm not alone." —Kevin

"Dr. Otani is a wealth of information. Bringing us to a happy state [and] spiritual aspects … I have gained a better sense of self through the experience." —Ron

References

Adler MG, and NS Fagley (February 2005). "Appreciation: Individual Differences in Finding Value and Meaning as a Unique Predictor of Subjective Well Being." *Journal of Personality*. 73 (1) : 79114.

Becker, Robert O., MD (1990). *Cross Currents*, Jeremy P. Tarcher, Inc. Los Angeles, CA.

Begley, Sharon (2007). *Change Your Mind, Change Your Brain*, Ballantine Books. New York, NY.

Birkmeyer NJ, Weinstein JN *Effective Practice Management* Sept/Oct. 1999

Casarjian, Robin (1992). *Forgiveness: A Bold Choice for a Peaceful Heart*, Bantam Books. New York, NY.

DA Christakis. *Pediatrics* April 2004, Vol. 113, Issue 4

Crum, Alia J., and Ellen J. Langer (2007). "Mind-Set Matters: Exercise and the Placebo Effect." *Psychological Science*. 18, no. 2.

Cutler, Howard C and H.H. Dalai Lama (1998). *The Art of Happiness*, Riverbend Books. New York, NY

Dean, Greg (2011). *Step By Step to Stand-up Comedy*. Silverlake Ebooks.

Dilts, Robert, Hallbom, Tim, and Suzi Smith (1990). *Beliefs: Pathway to Health & Well-Being*.
Metamorphous Press. Portland, OR.

Emmons RA, and ME McCullough (February 2003). "Counting Blessings versus Burdens: an Experimental Investigation of Gratitude and Subjective Well-Being in Daily Life" *Journal of Personality and Social Psychology*. 84 (2) : 37789.

Emmons, RA, McCullough, ME. *Journal of Personality and Social Psychology.* 84,377-389

Emoto, Masaru (2004). *The Hidden Messages of Water.* Beyond Words Publishing, Inc. Hillsboro, OR.

Epel ES et.al. PNAS Vol. 101 No. 49 17312-17315

Ericksson PS et. al. (1998) Nature Medicine (4) 1313-1317

Felitte, Vincent J.; Anda, Robert F.; et. al. (May 1998). "Relationship of Childhood Abuse and Household Dysfunction to Many of the Leading Causes of Death in Adults." *American Journal of Preventive Medicine.* Volume 14, Issue 4. Pages 245–258.

Fior J *J Cancer* 2014: 5(8) 715-719

Gage, F.H., van Praag, H., and G. Kempermann (1999). "Running Increases Cell Proliferation and Neurogenesis in Adult Mouse Dentate Gyrus." *Nature Neuroscience* Vol. 2. Pages 266–70.

Gertz, Kathryn Rose (June 2005). "Why Laughter Is Good For You." *Toastmaster Magazine.*

Glasser, William, MD (2003). *Warning: Psychiatry Can Be Hazardous To Your Mental Health.*
Harper Collins Publishers. New York, NY.

Goebel, Marion U., and Paul J. Mills (2000). "Acute Psychological Stress and Exercise and Changes in Peripheral Leukocyte Adhesion Molecule Expression and Density." *Psychosomatic Medicine* 62. Pages 664–670.

Gorman, James (July 2011). "Baboon Study Shows Benefit for Nice Guys, Who Finish 2nd." *The New York Times.*

Hawkins, David, MD, PhD (1995). *Power vs. Force.* Veritas Publishing. Sedona, AZ.

Jampolsky, Gerald (1985). *Good-bye to Guilt: Releasing Fear Through Forgiveness*. Bantam Books. New York, NY.

Johnson, Don Hanlon (2005). "Breathing, Moving, Sensing, and Feeling: Somatics and Integral Medicine."

Kaplan, Steve (2013). *The Hidden Tools of Comedy*. Michael Wiese Productions. Studio City, CA.

Klein, Allen (1989). *The Healing Power of Humor*. Jeremy P. Tarcher/Putnam. New York, NY.

Laibow, Rima (1999). "Clinical Applications: Medical Applications of Neurofeedback." *Introduction to Quantitative EEG and Neurofeedback*. J.R. Evans and A. Abarbanel. Academic Press (Elsevier). Burlington, MA.

Lipton, Bruce, PhD (2005). *Biology of Belief*. Hay House, Inc. Carlsbad, CA.
Luskin, Fred (2002). *Forgive For Good*. Harper Collins. New York, NY.
Marmot, M. G.; Davey Smith, G.; Stansfield, S.; et al. (1991). "Health Inequalities Among British Civil Servants: the Whitehall II Study." *Lancet* 337 (8754). Pages 1387–1393.

McEwen, Bruce S (July 2007). "Physiology and Neurobiology of Stress and Adaptation: Central Role of the Brain." *Physiological Reviews*. Volume 87, no. 3. Pages 873–904.

Mobbs D, Hagan C *PNAS* Nov.8, 2005, Vol.102, No. 45

Moseley, J.B.; O'Malley, K.; et. al. (2002). "A Controlled Trial of Arthroscopic Surgery for Osteoarthritis of the Knee." *New England Journal of Medicine*. 347 (2). Pages 81–88.

Niemi, Maj-Britt (February/March 2009). "Cure in the Mind" *Scientific American Mind*.

Rinpoche, Sogyal (2002). *The Tibetan Book of Living and Dying*. Harper Collins. New York, NY.

Sargent, Stacey (2013). *Inner Critic Inner Success*. Three-G Publishing. OH.

Schlitz, Marilyn, Amorok, Tina, and Micozzi, Marc S. *Consciousness and Healing*. Elsevier/Churchill Livingstone. Netherlands.

Schucman, Helen, and William Thetford (1992). *A Course In Miracles*. Foundation for Inner Peace. Mill Valley, CA.

Segerstrom S. Miller G Psycho Bull. 2004, Jul 130(4): 601- 630

Shively, Carol, and Jeanne M. Wallace (2001). "Social Status, Social Stress and Fat Distribution in Primates." *International Textbook of Obesity*.

C Stout, J Morrow.et.al. JAMA 188 (10) 845-849

Ting-Toomey, Stella, and Leeva Chung (2005). *Understanding Intercultural Communication*.
Oxford University Press, Inc. New York, NY.

Van Praag, Henrietta; Christie, B.R.; Sejnowski, T.J.; and Gage, F.H. (1999). "Running Enhances Neurogenesis, Learning and Long-Term Potentiation in Mice." *Proceedings of the National Academy of Science* 96. Pages 13427–31.

Wenner, Melinda (February/March 2009). "The Serious Need for Play." *Scientific American Mind*.

AM Wood, S Joseph, J Lloyd, S Atkins. *Journal of Psychosomatic Research*. Jan. 2009. Vol.66 Issue 1 pages 43-48

Young E, Akil H Neuropeptides 1985 Feb 5 (6-4); 545-8

Zukav, Gary (1979) *The Dancing Wu Li Masters* William Morrow and Company. New York, NY

CPSIA information can be obtained
at www.ICGtesting.com
Printed in the USA
LVOW13s1217201216
517998LV00002B/3/P

9 781457 551147